American Studies in India

Essays in History, Politics and Foreign Affairs

In the Same Series

Indian Perspectives on the U.S.: Literature and Foreign Affairs
P.M. Kamath and A.A. Mutalik Desai, ed.

American Literature Today
Suman Bala

Jewish American Writers
D. Venkateswarlu

American Drama
D. Venkateswarlu

The Novels of William Styron
S. Laxmana Murthy

The Novels of Bernard Malamud
M. Rajagopalachari

American Studies in India:

Essays in History, Politics and Foreign Affairs

Edited by

P.M. Kamath

PRESTIGE

Published by
Prestige Books
New Delhi 110 008

Distributed by
Intellectual Book Corner
23, Daryaganj, Ansari Road
New Delhi 110 002

1994
ISBN: 81-85218-84-6

Phototypesetting by
Pivot Computers
Delhi 110 006
Ph. 291 8404

Printed at
Mehra Offset Press
New Delhi 110 002

Contents

Preface

The present anthology includes 13 papers presented by members and presidential address delivered by me at the 27th Annual Conference of the Indian Association for American studies (IAAS) held at Goa University from March 29 to 31, 1993. The papers have been arranged on a thematic basis. A look at the past and the present of the IAAS shows that it has made significant progress in the publication of papers submitted by the scholars interested in American studies – broadly defined.

In 1987, I was able to get some selected papers dealing with Indo-US relations published by South Asian Publishers. On the occasion of the 27th Annual Conference, we were able to release a publication, *Indian Perspectives on the U.S.: Literature and Foreign Affairs* consisting of selected papers presented at the 26th Annual Conference held at Baroda. This collection included papers in the broad areas of literature and foreign affairs. This year we are able to present to our members two volumes one in the broad area of history and political science and another in the area of literature. I am sure this volume, addressed to a well-read and intelligent reader, will significantly enhance our understanding of complexities of American politics and foreign policy.

We, in the IAAS, are all thankful to Prestige Books, particularly to Dr. R.K. Dhawan and Dr. Suman Bala, for overseeing the prompt publication and making the volumes available in time for the release on the occasion of the opening day of the 28th Annual Conference of the IAAS on April 2, 1994.

P.M. KAMATH
President, IAAS

Contributors

Dipankar Basu, Darjeeling Govt. College, W.B.

Virbala Brahmabhatt, Maniben Nanavati Women's College, Bombay

Gitanjali Dash, Utkal University, Bhubaneswar

V.P. Gaur, B.I.T.S., Pilani

B.K. Gupta, B.I.T.S., Pilani

P.M. Kamath, University of Bombay, Bombay

Gajendra Kumar, R.D.S. College, Muzaffarpur

Harendra Mehta, C.H.M. College, Ulhasnagar

Dilip Mohite, M.S. University of Baroda

Umesh Patri, D.A.V. College, Koraput

Subhram Rajkhowa, Guwahati University, Assam

V.Y.D. Raman, S.V. University College, Tirupati

Winton S. Solberg, University of Illinois

Manoj Soni, S.P. University, Gujarat

Introduction

P.M. KAMATH

This collection of essays begins with a most appropriate paper on "What is American Studies?" by Winton U. Solberg, Professor Emeritus of History, University of Illinois at Urbana-champaign. He shows how the American studies grew as an academic discipline in the US after World War II. Developed as an area study, it moved from structuralism to post-structuralism and from modernism to post-modernism. Solberg argues that American studies with its basic inter-disciplinary approach destroyed borders separating traditional disciplines. Though American studies in the US dealt mainly with subjects like history and literature, to understand American culture and civilization, it also drew from other disciplines like art, architecture, law, politics, philosophy, religion and sociology.

What is American Studies? The question is answered by Solberg by stating that it "is a systematic and disciplined effort to understand the empirical reality of society and culture in the United States. The best approach is through the combined study of American intellectual and cultural history and American literature."

In India however, the concept of integrated and inter-disciplinary study of American culture and civilization has not been able to develop. In India it is mainly a study of America—its literature, history, politics and other aspects of life and society. The earliest beginning of the study of America began with the study of American history. Gajendra Kumar, in his paper on "American Intellectual History: Trends in Historiography" discusses, though briefly, how American intellectual history came to be influenced by the American studies movement in the 1930s. In the process it gained popularity but lost its coherence. It is this limitation of interdisciplinary approach and consequent lack of job opportunities for the scholars specializing in American studies, that is a deterring factor in the growth of American studies in India.

It is the above reason that has led Indian Americanists to take recourse to studies in individual fields of humanities or social sciences.

Umesh Patri in his paper "Hindu Influence on Henry David Thoreau" argues that Thoreau found the concept of man in Christianity and Hinduism as diametrically opposed to each other; the former sees man as a born sinner whereas the latter takes him to be potentially divine. Thoreau had arrived at this conclusion by his study of Hindu scriptures like the *Bhagavad Gita*, the *Manu Smriti*, the *Puranas* and the *Upanishads.* Thoreau was also far more influenced by Hinduism than Emerson. Thoreau, Patri says, was a *Karma Yogi*, *Jnana Yogi* and also a *Raja Yogi.*

While in philosophy and culture India has a lot to offer to the US, in the present times, India offers its trained manpower to the US. In a sense, it is India's foreign aid to the US. With over one million people of Indian origin settled in the US, India has also provided Indians as well as Americans, a new field of study—Indian-Americans and societal, cultural changes in them.

In this background Virbala Brahmabhatt focuses narrowly on "The Role of Indian Women Immigrants in the US." Early women who went to the US to study like Anandibai Joshi or Pandita Ramabai went to return. But in the post-independent years, the first phase of immigration began in 1965 when a large number of women went to the US as wives of Indians settled there and by and large, confined themselves as housewives. But in the second phase that began a decade later, larger number of women went to the US who started working in small and big jobs like managing hotels and motels, shop-keeping, medicine, teaching and scores of other jobs. Indian women have come out rapidly from their conservative environment in the liberal atmosphere of the US.

Of course, the first generation of Indian-Americans has established over five hundred associations to preserve their traditional ways of life in the wake of younger generation going the American way. The associations still remain relevant, as more Indians immigrate to settle in the US as the economic and social conditions in India continue to worsen everyday and Indian youth looks for greener pastures.

An important reason for the better-educated Indians to look at the US as a nation where they can better utilize their talents and also improve their economic status is the growing ethnic and communal strife in India. P.M. Kamath in his essay "A Case for Presidential Government in India" (Presidential Address, 27th Annual Conference) argues that India faces communalization of politics, political instability and threat to national unity and integrity as three major challenges.

In the contemporary times it is possible to look to the US for new visions to improve our system of government. Kamath argues that a presidential system is far more effective in keeping a heterogeneous society like India together through a nationally elected Chief Executive.

Presidential system not only will help curb growing communalism (in the sense of seeking votes on grounds of caste and religious loyalties of individuals) but will also help to promote a two-party system. The changeover to presidential system would also help to achieve a reasonable degree of political stability and control political defections. It will also make federal system more federal through directly elected governors in the states.

The Presidency is the heart of the American political system. The next two essays deal with the issues relating to the Presidential elections of 1992. V.Y.D. Raman, in his paper "Vietnam in the Presidential Election of 1992," focuses on a single factor of the influence of Clinton's dodging of draft during the Vietnam War and as a student in the UK joining in public protest against the US. Emotional issues like 'why should he be permitted to dodge the draft when kids from ghettos were dying in minefields' were raised during the elections. This question made many supporters of Bill Clinton take a second look at his candidacy. Stalwarts of the Vietnam War days, like Robert McNamara, came to the rescue of Clinton who wrote that in Clinton's time, college students were opposed to the War. McNamara added: "I knew then and I know now, the anguish of those who honestly—and sincerely and perhaps correctly—opposed the war."

Subhram Rajkhowa, on the other hand, discusses in his paper "American Presidential Elections, 1992," how various new devices in electioneering were used by all the main contestants, Bill Clinton, George Bush and Ross Perot, like phone-in and phone-out and negative campaigning on TV. The democratic party continues to suffer from the voter-divisive factor of advocacy of conflicting interests by special interest groups. President Bill Clinton owes his electoral victory to heavy support by some special interest groups like those representing women and Gays. But more important is the fact of the presence of a third candidate Ross Perot, in a basically two-party system. Perot secured 19 percent of popular votes against Clinton's 43 per cent and Bush's 38 per cent. It is clear that Perot who withdrew from contest in July 92 only to reenter in October, succeeded to take away a large chunk of disillusioned independent voters. His absence in the race could have tilted the results against Clinton. Bill Clinton has become the 42nd President, when the world politics has undergone radical changes with the end of cold war after the disintegration of the Soviet Union. What affects the other countries of the world, including India, is the way in which the US conducts its foreign relations. The next six papers in this collection concern themselves with different aspects of American foreign policy. Harendra Mehta attempts to discuss "The Basic Dilemma of American Foreign

Policy." He identifies American idealistic commitment to humanism expressed in the preamble of the constitution and the hegemonistic protection of power in the post-cold war period in reality, as the basic dilemma of American foreign policy. This dilemma in practice has disabled the US to comprehend the cultures of other nations, including that of India, economic problems of the Third World and has legitimized violence in foreign affairs.

The American foreign policy did not face these problems for over one hundred fifty years since America was founded as a republic in 1787. It strictly adhered to George Washington's clarion call in his farewell address to the nation to avoid entanglement in foreign alliances. As a result, the US followed a policy of isolationism. In effect, it did not get involved in European politics or was marginally involved.

But after World War II, the US emerged as a strong, and powerful super power only to be challenged, ironically, by its war-time ally—the Soviet Union. The cold war continued until the disintegration of the Soviet Union in December 1991. V.P. Gaur in his paper on "End of the Cold War and American Foreign Policy" gives sound advice to the US that though it has emerged as a super power, it should not try to isolate Russia, if it wants to prevent reemergence of another cold war. The cost of maintaining hegemonistic status will be too high. Instead, it will be in American interest to strengthen the UN and act under its umbrella.

This is particularly relevant in the context made out by Gitanjali Dash in her paper on "US Foreign Policy after the Cold War." She argues that the US has emerged as the only super power at a time when it has also become economically a declining power. This is particularly true in relation to two of its World War II enemies turned post-war allies—Germany and Japan. Though unified Germany is facing some problems of adjustments between east and west, Germany has emerged as a formidable economic challenger to the US. Similarly, Japan too has emerged as an economic super power.

Dipankar Basu specifically discusses the effects of unification of Germany and the break-up of the Soviet Union on the US foreign policy. The US was a champion of the European unity espousing greater economic and political integration of Europe. It was a supporter rather promoter of the idea European Community (EC) during the cold war period as a bulwark against the expansionist Soviet Union. The Maastricht treaty of December 1991 had even spoken of common defence and foreign policy of EC. However, once the Soviet Union distintegrated, the US saw the development of a unified Europe as a possible economic threat. The earlier dream of a European man was practically shattered with the failure of the European Monetary Union to take off.

The United Kingdom has always cherished her special relationship with the US rather than integration with Europe. Now that the Soviet threat is no longer a basic input in the making of European foreign policy, the UK does not want to move towards a common defence or foreign policy. The UK is undoubtedly blessed by the US in this direction.

Does the US promote a free market or free trade between a unified Europe and the US? The formation of NAFTA does not show that it is really committed to free trade concept on a trans-Atlantic lines. However, at the same time, the US wants to retain and expand the role of NATO though its original *raison de'tre* no longer exists. NATO's recent decision to admit East European states like Poland and Hungary into NATO is a confirmation of this trend. This might eventually force Russia to take an antagonistic stance towards the US and NATO, giving rise to the emergence of cold war.

Manoj Soni in his paper on "Rethinking the Superness of American Power" also tries to understand these very issues in the context of international relations theory. He examines how Gorbachev period saw the withdrawal of the Soviet Union as a challenger to the US which enabled the US to emerge as the single most powerful power giving an illusion of unipolar world. He also analyzes emergence of Japan as a competitor to the US in economic world.

Dilip Mohite in his paper "The Post-Cold War World Order: Some Emerging Trends" discusses at length how the end of cold war has led to the emergence of a unipolar world. Despite the apparent unipolarity of the existing international system, regional issues like ethnic conflicts, environmental degradation, diffusion of military capability from North to South continue to dominate the global agenda.

B.K. Gupta in his paper on "The End of the Cold War and New Challenges to USA" discusses new challenges faced by the US after the end of the cold war. He lists international terrorism, violation of human rights and use of force in the international relations in the changed context as main challenges. These are also the issues affecting Indo-US relations in the last decade of the twentieth century.

What is American Studies?

WINTON U. SOLBERG

Understanding any society is a complex undertaking, as scholars know. India is a diverse, complex, and ancient civilization; to comprehend it challenges Americans. The United States is much younger than India, but it too is diverse and complex, and Indians can find America difficult to understand.

What is the best way to gain knowledge and appreciation of the United States? If one answers, by the academic discipline of American Studies, the question arises, what is American Studies?

I would like to deal with this problem by exploring the origins of American Studies, discussing the development of the field, and describing the recent influence of poststructuralism and postmodernism. Then I shall draw a conclusion. This is a large agenda.

The Origins of American Studies as an Academic Discipline

The institutional context for the origins of American Studies was the disciplinary and departmental structure of American universities. The university rather than the college became the characteristic form of higher education in America in the late nineteenth century. Universities needed an appropriate structure in which to teach and conduct research, and as such broad areas of study as the natural sciences, the social sciences, and the humanities became specialized, departments became the basic units within the university—biology, physics, history, literature, and others. Departments developed strength and autonomy, and each was determined to protect its own turf.

This rigid division along disciplinary lines had both strengths and weaknesses, and in time scholars sought to transcend the limitations by an interdisciplinary approach. This led to employment of intersecting approaches. In the sciences the result was such fields as biochemistry and biophysics; in the social sciences it was area studies programs such as Asian Studies and Russian Studies. American Studies was a pioneer in interdisciplinary programs. Scholars at prestige universities led the way.

At Harvard University Kenneth B. Murdoch and Francis O. Matthiesen, both in American literature, were pioneers. At Yale University the innovators were Ralph H. Gabriel and Stanley Williams, in American history and American literature respectively.

The founders had a clear vision of their enterprise. They regarded history and literature as the core of American Studies, and they emphasized intellectual and cultural history, which is concerned with seminal ideas in social context. Taking ideas seriously, intellectual history investigates the intersection between basic ideas such as Calvinism, democracy, liberty, romanticism, Darwinism, Marxism, and Freudianism and the culture in which they operate.

Developments in Later Years

In addition to history and literature, American Studies recognized other disciplines, including art, architecture, law, politics, philosophy, religion, and sociology, as contributing to the understanding of American culture. Moreover, scholars enlarged the field of American Studies by employing a variety of integrating themes. Among the leading examples of influential books on American Studies that employed some principle of integration are Henry Nash Smith, *Virgin Land: The American West as Symbol and Myth* (1950), John William Ward, *Andrew Jackson: Symbol for an Age* (1955), R.W.B. Lewis, *The American Adam* (1959), and Leo Marx, *The Machine in the Garden: Technology and the Pastoral Idea in America* (1969).

When intellectual history ceased to serve an integrating function and when scholars lacked a convincing integrating principle, a wide variety of disparate works in American Studies appeared. These ranged from the significant to the silly, as anyone who has chaired the program committee or attended regional and national meetings of American Studies associations will testify.

As a result of this sprawl, American Studies lost status as an academic discipline. Scholars in departments that possessed sharp disciplinary contours criticized American Studies as lacking scholarly rigor. Their attitude seemed justified when undergraduate enrollments swamped American Studies, convincing observers that students viewed the courses as easy—a "snap." To retain the integrity of American Studies and to challenge the better students, many colleges established honors programs in American Studies.

As courses proliferated on American campuses, a variety of new interdisciplinary programs arose in response to perceived needs. African-American Studies, Hispanic-American Studies, Native American Studies,

Gender Studies, Feminist Theory, and Film Studies all competed with American Studies for students.

Meanwhile, a debate over the purpose of the university began on American campuses. Did universities exist primarily for the transmission and reproduction of culture, or for the criticism and recreation of culture? Two schools of thought provided answers. One saw the study of cultural representations as a hermeneutical struggle, a problem of interpretation. The other saw the study of cultural representations as a political struggle and valued ideology as a unifying concept.

This debate was carried by traditional humanists versus partisans of poststructuralism and postmodernism. Devotees of these new isms had their greatest impact on literature, especially in English departments, with a lesser influence on history and history departments. Poststructuralism and postmodernism have close affinities, but they differ and should be examined separately and in historical perspective.

The Impact of Poststructuralism and Postmodernism

The scientific revolution that culminated in Newton gave people a new understanding of the physical universe, and in its wake thinkers from Vico in the eighteenth century to Piaget in the twentieth century strove to create a science of human society. Structuralism, their handiwork, is a way of thinking about the world that is primarily concerned with the perception and description of structures. This new doctrine crystallized in the early twentieth century, and many of its central concepts were further developed in the study of language and the study of man. Ferdinand Saussure, a Swiss linguist, whose *Course in General Linguistics* was posthumously published in 1915, laid the foundations for structural linguistics. Claude Levi-Strauss, the French anthropologist, drew upon this body of knowledge in his studies of kinship, myth-making, and the savage mind of primitive peoples. His publications in the 1950s and early 1960s helped consolidate structuralism as an intellectual discipline.

According to structuralism, which represented a momentous historic shift in thought, every individual's perception contains a bias that affects what is perceived. We construct the world as we perceive it, and in so doing we construct ourselves. Since objective perception of discrete entities is not possible, the relationship between observer and observed becomes the stuff of reality itself. The notion that the true nature of things lies in the relationships which we construct and perceive between them constitutes the first principle of structuralist thought. Linguistic signs are characterized in terms of the relationship between a signifier, a concept or a word, like *tree*, and a signified, the sound image made by a word like *tree*. This relationship is purely arbitrary; there is no appeal to a reality beyond the structure itself. Words function without reference to the real existence of the referent. The so-called objective world does not exist but is manufactured by us within and through our total pattern of behavior.

Poststructuralism arose in France in the 1960s and 1970s out of the tension between structuralism and phenomenology. It does not use structural linguistics. Yet the two movements share many similarities. Both deconstruct the conceptions by which we understand the human. Both share an antipathy to an overall pattern in history. Both criticize meaning; but structuralism maintains a balance between signifier and signified, stressing the unity of the sign, while poststructuralism makes the signifier dominant and sees no correspondence between propositions and reality. And both criticize the main tradition in Western philosophy—metaphysics, causality, and truth.

Jacques Derrida and Michel Foucault, philosophers who drew heavily on Freud, Nietzsche, Husserl, and Heidegger, are the gurus of poststructuralism. Derrida argues that there are certain long-standing constraints in Western philosophy that constitute hidden contracts between bodies of knowledge, institutions, and power; these are inscribed in and demonstrated by texts. Thus philosophy cannot be separated from cultural, political, or other forces contending for power. The continued authority of certain texts through time is not validated by these outside forces but rather by misreading of the texts themselves. Social ideologies elevate certain meanings to privileged positions. Misreadings are possible because texts contain opposed, undecidable meanings. Deconstruction, the method advocated to unpack the undecidable meanings in order to grasp their contradictory determinations, challenges their current readings. Close reading reveals binary opposites within a text. Language is unstable; words need to be put "under erasure," which reveals that meaning is what the sign is not. Deconstruction shows that texts fail by their own criteria. It disseminates meanings and interpretations not consciously intended by the author. Derrida stresses intertextuality: every text should be read in light of other texts. Above all, one should avoid assertions about truth.

Foucault, who left philosophical analysis for intellectual history, went through many stages of thought. Foucault I was an archeologist of the human sciences who presented a subversive history of modern ideas about man. Since Foucault acknowledged no universal norms, he was unable to make judgements or take political positions. Foucault II was a microphysicist of power. After the massive student demonstrations of May 1968 he examined the modern technology of social control. Since he described every political regime as a power relation, the question arose as to what grounds justified taking a stand against any regime. Foucault III undertook a comparative study of pagan morality of the Greeks and Christian morality with the aim of clarifying our moral assumptions about the autonomous individual: should one aim at happiness or obedience to the divine law? Foucault IV was a philosopher who inspired the other Foucaults.

Poststructuralism spread from France to the United States, where it has enjoyed its greatest success. The American career of poststructuralism began at Johns Hopkins University in 1966. Derrida, the final speaker in a conference designed to celebrate the advent of structuralism, declared that structuralism was finished. It was doomed because one could not study the structure of a text if that structure lacked a center or organizing principle to give it coherence. The problem began when "language invaded the universal problematic, the moment when, in the absence of a center or origin, everything became discourse." Nothing exists outside of language, Derrida declared; no things or ideas exist except in words, and words have an autonomous existence because they are grounded in nothing else.

Derrida and deconstruction became intellectually fashionable in America starting in the late 1960s. An academic enterprise, it made its presence felt primarily in literary studies. At first an anti-establishment movement, it attracted some of the best and brightest minds, and when senior professors in reputable universities became devotees, it achieved institutional prestige and power. Its center was at Yale, where the leading proponents were J. Hillis Miller; Derrida himself, who was often a visiting professor at Yale; and Paul de Man. Other focal points were Johns Hopkins, Cornell, Duke, and later the University of California at Irvine.

Deconstruction also spread to other academic disciplines. At a biblical studies conference in 1986, one panelist prresented a paper entitled "Deconstruction and the Parables of Jesus," and another panelist countered with "Deconstructing 'Deconstruction and the Parables of Jesus' . . . or Does the Cat Perpetually Chase Its Tail?" William Dean defended the "deconstructivism" of Derrida in *History Making History: The New Historicism in American Religious Thought* (1988), and Stephen D. Moore displayed a heavy debt to Derrida and deconstruction in *Literary Criticism and the Gospels: The Theoretical Challenge* (1989).

In 1988 the Museum of Modern Art in New York held a show of "Deconstructivist Architecture" in 1988. "Deconstruction," wrote a curator, "gains all its force by challenging the very values of harmony, unity, and stability, and proposing instead a different view of structure; the view that the flaws are intrinsic to the structure." A deconstructive architect, the curator added, is "not one who dismantles buildings, but one who locates the inherent dilemmas within buildings. The deconstructive architect puts the pure forms of the architectural tradition on the couch and identifies the symptoms of a repressed impurity. The impurity is drawn to the surface by a combination of gentle coaxing and violent torture: the form is interrogated."

Deconstruction was the driving intellectual force of the "Critical Legal Studies" movement. Its adherents emphasized the doctrine of indeterminacy derived from deconstruction. They viewed law as the instrument of the ideology of the ruling class and sought to demystify the law. They approached the law as a branch of literature awaiting deconstruction. Considering all texts indeterminate, they noted that the "fundamental contradiction" at the core of any normative concept cause it to break down into antithetical sense. This contradiction allows a judge to choose either of two diametrically opposed interpretations in any case that comes before the court. Thus, there can be no criteria for determining the correctness of a judicial decision, and the rational basis for law is fatally compromised. The Critical Legal Studies movement deeply divided the Harvard Law School faculty, made inroads in other law schools, and influenced a number of younger scholars. The title of Gillian Rose's book, *Dialectic of Nihilism: Post-Structuralism and the Law* (1984), is suggestive of the movement. A Yale law professor described the CLS critique of law as intellectually without merit and politically irresponsible. Most law professors would agree.

One need not multiply examples to demonstrate the pervasive influence of Derrida in the American university. "America *is* deconstruction," Derrida announced as early as 1983. The United States, he added, "is that historical space which today, in all its dimensions and through all its power plays, reveals itself as being undeniably the most sensitive, receptive, or responsive space of all to the themes and effects of deconstruction."

A number of reasons help explain this triumph. Some believe that deconstruction flourishes because it capitalizes on a crisis of authority and a crisis of faith. It appeals to the temper of the times, emphasizing negative rather than positive modes of thought. Some say that deconstruction exemplifies cult-formation as a method of prevailing in the university. Once deconstruction became orthodoxy, young academics saw that their careers depended upon becoming disciples in the faith. Others note that the foes of deconstruction are pluralists who willingly accommodate rival doctrines. Still others think that novelty was an important source of deconstruction's appeal. As the New Criticism ran its course, scholars willingly embraced new theories. Finally, some view deconstruction as the revenge of the counterculture. Unable to break the structures of state power, rebels of the late 1960s set out to subvert the structures of language. In this view, deconstruction is an episode in the history of "the youth culture" rather than in the history of ideas.

The doctrine of deconstruction is a force to reckon with, but its method and concepts have polarized the academy. On the one hand it has exerted a beneficial influence on various academic disciplines. Deconstructionists have challenged old assumptions and insisted on looking at familiar ideas with fresh eyes. They have dissolved the borders that traditionally separate disciplines, explored the relation between language and meaning, and focused on the margins rather than the center of the text. All this has brought rich rewards. On the other hand deconstruction has aroused strong opposition. It has an antic side. Geoffrey Hartman called it "Derridaism," and M.H. Abrams, the distinguished Cornell critic, labeled deconstruction as "the serious philosophy of the absurd." Deconstruction also has a hard, rigorous, dogmatic side that gives it the character of an antitheological theology. It emphasizes criticism over literature and theory over criticism, sharpening the disjunction between the word and the world. It undermines the traditional canon in a way that helps provoke Allan Bloom's *Closing of the American Mind* (1987) and E.D. Hirsch's *Cultural Literacy* (1987), both of which proved enormously popular. Finally, with its anti-humanist and anti-rational program, deconstruction is profoundly subversive.

Poststructuralism is closely associated with postmodernism. These two terms refer to distinct but overlapping modes of discourse. Postmodernism is variously described as the cultural correlate of late capitalism; as the cultural correlate of post-industrial society in which knowledge is the principal form of production; as contemporary culture without reference to political and economic determinants; and an anti-intellectualism that threatens the humanism and enlightenment of modern culture. Postmodernism and poststructuralism share a concern with the creation of culture, that is, the forms of social consciousness that give meaning to the condition and public expression of human behavior. The creation of culture is often contested terrain, especially when it threatens established forms of domination. Postmodernism is concerned with how the "culture industry" of a country reproduces culture, transforming it from something genuine into a spurious thing that satisfies the needs of consumer capitalism. Postmodernists pose questions that attract the attention of poststructuralists, and they have appropriated the writings of Derrida and Foucault to provide answers.

Most historians have not yet directly confronted the issues raised by poststructuralism and postmodernism. They tend to dismiss the discourse as philosophical tracts of interest to theoreticians rather than to practitioners of the profession. Modernist history, or traditional history, like postmodernist history, is relativistic, but its relativism is rooted in reality. Modernist history is skeptical of absolute truth but not of contingent, incremental truths. It does not deny the reality of the past itself. The modernist historian reads and writes history with scrupulous regard for the historicity and actuality of the past. Historians have always known that postmodernism professes to have just discovered: that any work of history is vulnerable because of the fallibility of the historical record on which it is based, the selectivity inherent in the writing of history, and the fallibility and subjectivity of the historian. Traditional historians have known that every historical work is necessarily imperfect and partial. Historians have also known that they themselves act and think in their own present. Every historian is a product of his age. Yet this awareness of the frailty, fallibility, and relativism of the historical enterprise is very different from the message of postmodernism. In history, postmodernism is a denial of reality of the past apart from what the historian chooses to make of it. Thus it is a denial of any objective truth about the past. Postmodernism presumes that all of history is fatally flawed and that because there is no absolute, total truth, there can be no partial, contingent truth. Postmodernism presupposes that because it is impossible to attain great truths, it is futile and baneful to aspire to them. Traditional history put a premium on a methodology that went into what was called the canon of evidence. This positivistic approach respected facts and documentation. The prevailing ideal was objectivity in the sense of unbiased truth. This standard was the norm of the historical profession in to the late 1960s, when Derrida and Foucault postmodernized it.

Postmodernists attack modernist or traditional history as uncritical. They deem modernist history as spurious because it conceals its ideological structure behind footnotes and a pretence of facts. To demystify this history, postmodernism has to expose not only its ideology—the hegemonic, privileged, patriarchal interests served by this history—but also its methodology, the scholarly apparatus that gives it a specious credibility. This is the agenda of postmodernist history: to free history from the shackles of an authoritarian ideology and to release it from the constraints of delusive methodology. The ultimate aim is to liberate us all from the coercive ideas of reality and truth.

Narrative history—narrativity—is for postmodernists the primary culprit. The belief that history is narrative depends on such arbitrary conventions as chronology, causality, and collectivity, and it takes the form of a logical, orderly structure of discourse that is presumed to correspond to the reality of the past. All this is anathema to postmodernism, which believes that history is a fictional, rhetorical, literary, and aesthetic creation of the historian.

The leading postmodernist philosopher of history is Hayden V. White. White took a doctorate at the University of Michigan with a dissertation on papal leadership in the twelfth century. A European intellectual historian who has closely studied Vico, White taught at four institutions before becoming professor of the history of consciousness at the University of California at Santa Cruz. White's books include *Metahistory: The Historical Imagination in Nineteenth-Century Europe* (1973), *Tropics of Discourse: Essays in Cultural Criticism* (1978), and *The Content of the Form: Narrative Discourse and Historical Representation* (1987). White's interest is more philosophical than historical and more literary than philosophical. His *Metahistory* opens with a chapter entitled "The Poetics of History," and each of his subjects from Hegel to Croce represents an aspect of the historical imagination.

For White, there is no distinction between history and philosophy or between history and literature. All of history, in his and the postmodernist view, is aesthetic and philosophic, its only meaning being that which the historian chooses to give it in accordance with his own sensibility. An event in the past is a text to be interpreted by the historian much as a poem is interpreted by a critic. And, like any literary text, the historical text is indeterminate and contradictory, so that it can be "textualized" and "retextualized" at will. The "text" is a nose of wax in the hands of the creative historian.

In postmodernist history, as in poststructuralist literary criticism, theory has become a calling in itself. So there are professors of history who do not write about actual historical events but devote their careers to speculation about the nature of history in general. And truth gives way to fiction. In his presidential address to the American Historical Association in 1975, Gordon Wright told fellow historians that "our search for truth ought to be quite consciously suffused by a commitment to some deeply held humane values." But times change. The philosopher Richard Rorty recently reported, with satisfaction, that it was getting more and more difficult to find "a real live metaphysical prig" who believes in such outmoded ideas as "reality" and "truth." The disdain for truth as a guiding rule of historical scholarship was illustrated by a controversy that erupted in 1985 over a book on the Weimar Republic by a young Princeton historian, David Abraham. Several eminent historians severely criticized Abraham for misquotations, faulty citations, and unwarranted deductions from the sources. Abraham defended himself, and some reputable historians came to his aid. One of his defenders denounced as naive those who believed in "the absolute certitude of historical fact"; he went on to insist that the "historical imagination" is central to any historical work, adding that this involves a process of "imaginative creation" which goes well beyond documents and facts. Postmodernists scorn "facticity" and deride those who respect factual accuracy as "vulgar factologists."

Modernist historians have always recognized the role of the imagination in the writing of history, but they have emphasized the need to put the imagination under strict constraints with a view to recording truth rather than fiction. Postmodernist historians, liberated from fact fetishism and persuaded of the fictive nature of all history, make historiography another genre of fiction. White's "metahistory" has now been redefined as "historiographic metafiction." Simon Schama, a Harvard historian, has introduced entirely fictional characters in what might appear to be a conventional history, identifying them as pure inventions only in an "Afterword."

Postmodernism appeals to the political imagination as well as the creative imagination. Some Marxists and old-fashioned radicals are suspicious of postmodernism as being apolitical, passive, and thus conservative. Jurgen Habermas considers Foucault neo-conservative because he offers no alternative to capitalism. The British Marxist critic Terry Eagleton says that since postmodernism commits you to affirming nothing, "it is as injurious as blank ammunition." Others see postmodernism as peculiarly congenial to such post-Marxist forms of radicalism as anti-racism, anti-sexism, and environmentalism, the currently fashionable protest ideologies of the American academic world.

Postmodernism is avowedly far more radical than either Marxism or these new protest ideologies, since it repudiates the Enlightenment principles of knowledge and rationality as well as rejecting the "discipline" of society and authority. In denying any reality apart from language, postmodernism aims to subvert the structure of society together with the structure of language. This is the explicit agenda of Foucault and Derrida, and it is less insistent but no less explicit in the work of Hayden White.

White repudiates conservative and Marxist historiography alike, but he echoes the familiar Marxist theory in explaining traditional history as a reflection of the class interests of bourgeoisie. His own relativism, he protests, is not conducive to the kind of nihilism that invites revolutionary activism of a particularly irresponsible sort. He describes his relativism as a counsel of tolerance rather than license. Rather than by revolution he proposes to subvert the social hierarchy by rejecting the conventional discipline of history—narrativity, objectivity, rules of evidence, and the rest of the "bourgeois ideology of realism." Only such a utopian, eschatological view of history, writes White, is consistent with "the kind of politics that is based on a vision of a perfected society."

In the vocabulary of postmodernism this anarchic view of history is translated as "indeterminacy," which is a standing invitation to creation out of nothing. With traditional history discredited, the historian finds a blank slate on which he can write whatever interpretation he likes. Thus the principle of indeterminacy lends itself to the determinacy of race, class, and gender. By deconstructing the "texts" of all previous histories, new histories can be created in accord with the political and ideological dispositions of their creators.

As Gertrude Himmelfarb observes, the political potential of postmodernism has been seized most enthusiastically by feminist historians, who find the old Marxism and some forms of the new radicalism unresponsive to their concerns. Thus, many postmodernist historians are feminists, and postmodernism figures prominently in feminist history. Joan W. Scott explains this political affinity as follows: "A more radical feminist politics (and a more radical feminist history) seems to me to require a more radical epistemology. Precisely because it addresses questions of epistemology, relates the status of all knowledge, links knowledge and power, and theorizes these in terms of the operations of difference, I think post-structuralism (or at least some of the approaches generally associated with Michel Foucault and Jacques Derrida) can offer feminism a powerful analytic perspective." As Himmelfarb notes, feminist history is profoundly subversive, not only of traditional history but of earlier varieties of women's history. The new feminist history demands that all of history be rewritten from a consciously feminist perspective. Thus feminist history requires a radical epistemology, and it becomes an instrument for feminist power.

If history is an instrument in the struggle for power, then every ethnic, racial, religious, sexual, national, ideological and other interest group will attempt to use it to further its own agenda. This idea is now being affirmed in the name of "multiculturalism," a concept that has become "politically correct" in American universities. People now celebrate five ethnic groups in the United States: Euro-Americans, Asian-Americans, Hispanic-Americans, Afro-Americans, and Native Americans. Multiculturalism has the effect of politicizing history. Worse, it dehumanizes the people who are the subjects of history. To particularize history to the point where they share no common history, have no cultural unity, as Arthur Schlesinger observes in *The Disuniting of America* (1922), is to fragment history to the point that it lacks meaning. From a postmodernist perspective, this is good, since it destroys hegemony and decenters the universalizing "logocentric" and "phallocentric" history that is decried as the evil of modernity.

Postmodernism is less prevalent among historians than among literary critics. Yet it exercises a disproportionate influence in history because it tends to attract many bright young people and offers to liberate historians from the hard discipline of traditional historical methodology. This methodological liberation is occurring, and it may prove to be the most lasting influence of postmodernism on the history profession.

As for poststructuralism and postmodernism themselves, there are grounds for concluding that they are just another of those intellectual fashions that seize academia from time to time. Existentialism had its vogue, and in France, deconstruction is already *passe*. In America, there are signs of disaffection with poststructuralism and postmodernism in history, literature, philosophy, and legal studies. The appeal of novelty wears off, the young rebel, and today's vanguard becomes tomorrow's rearguard. The counter-revolution is already underway in the form of the "New Historicism," a linguistic version of Marxism which interprets "cultural productions" as the symbolic forms of "material productions" and "social relations."

What, Then, Is American Studies?

Poststructuralism and postmodernism have left deep traces in the United States, and because of their impact on literature and history they have inevitably shaped the way American Studies is studied and taught. But let us suppose that poststructuralism and postmodernism gradually fade away. What then? What will serve as a unifying approach in studying American thought and culture? What is American Studies?

My answer is, American Studies is a systematic and disciplined effort to understand the empirical reality of society and culture in the United States. The best approach is through the combined study of American intellectual and cultural history and American literature. These are necessary but not sufficient conditions for understanding the United States. One can usefully appropriate some of the insights of poststructuralism to enrich American Studies, but it is important to remember that there is such a phenomenon as American culture and that scholars should study it objectively and with confidence that they can discover at least some contingent truths about this reality.

American Intellectual History: Trends in Asia

GAJENDRA KUMAR

John Higham has described intellectual historian as an amateur philosopher. It is so because he has to focus attention "on the experience of thought rather than external behaviour. For the intellectual historian, not culture, politics or art but state of mind make the foreground of interest and the focus of curiosity."[1] Although general approach towards the nature of intellectual history has by and large been eclectic, the ultimate objective of the intellectual historian is to provide an explanation of the spirit of a given age.

Intellectual historians of the nineteenth and early twentieth centuries like Leslie Stephen, Alfred N. Whitehead concerned themselves with the growth of inner life of an age. They sought to demonstrate the spirit of their age, taking recourse to assessment of a cross-section of articulate representative group. In fact, in doing so, the intellectual historian of that period usurped for themselves the task of philosophers. It will be perhaps more appropriate to state that when the pragmatic thinkers could not work out a solid framework for their belief in metaphysical format, they solicited guidance from intellectual history to have a proper appreciation of the importance of ideas around them.

The nineteenth century intellectual historians may be criticized on the ground that they seldom took the trouble of explaining as to what constituted thought and how it interacted with events. However, it does not deprive them of the acclaim they so richly deserve. As a matter of fact, they undertook pioneer work on a grand and generous scale, thereby ensuring that their work would merit more concrete and serious considerations in subsequent times.

The traditional conception of intellectual history came under serious attack by the protagonists of "the New History" in the 1920s. Intellectual history moved beyond the domain of amateurish philosophers, assuming for themselves tasks of intellectual historians. Precisely speaking, it became a pursuit of professional historians, having affiliation with particular academic disciplines.

Led by James Harvey Robinson,[2] this genre of professional historians proceeded to make history more pervasive and purposeful to the realities of post-war democratic fabric. Instead of endorsing the prevalent philosophic attitude towards intellectual history, they began to cherish down-to-earth perception of intellectual history.

The volume of literature produced by supporters of the New History virtually amounted to revolt against formalism. Their writings became comprehensive enough to provide little scope for sustained analysis of ideas. Moreover, they were influenced by materialistic interpretation of history and shared the view of Richard Hofstadter that transformation in the structure of social ideas closely follow the change of pattern in the economic and social pattern.[3]

In India, in due course, the dynastic history writing gave way to the history of masses. In the similar fashion, the new historians contributed to broad-based kind of writing of intellectual history. They almost accused the traditional intellectual historians of being aristocratic in their writings by discarding discussions on aspects of life, concerning common faith.

In fact, they sought to make intellectual history more democratic and appreciable by integrating intellectuals with common man. Their outstanding achievements lay in the craftsmanship of linking high culture with popular belief.

Acknowledging the contribution of New Historians towards intellectual history writing, John Higham has aptly surmised: "Led by Merle Curtis and Ralph H. Gabriel, historians showed that intellectual history of democratic society where no class lines set natural limits to the circulation of ideas, calls for close attention to the process of popular diffusion and intellectual crystallization."[4]

However, in their quest for making history, a unifying discipline, they became casual in retaining the inherent intelligibility and importance of intellectual history as such. In quest of a pragmatic synthesis, the New History tended to squeeze all ideas into a matrix of events and institutions.

Although protagonists of the New History brought intellectual history into the mainstream of professional historical interest and inspired abundance of valuable research, they did not care for the interpretation of the spirit of the age. Further in their zeal for comprehensiveness they "dissipated the force and coherence that the old intellectual history had at its best."

Certain distinct features of the New History viz. (i) pragmatism, (ii) anti-formalism and (iii) instrumental consideration considerably influenced non-professionals. Scholars belonging to other disciplines sought to get away with compartmentalization through intellectual history. It resulted in pouring of literature that was more technical and less historical.

After the 1930s the American intellectual history came to be influenced by the American Studies Movement. Scholars of literature were the prime movers of American Studies programme and they had many points of convergence with the New Historians. Intellectual history appealed to them as vital and viable medium for effecting a synthesis of heterogeneous materials. Intellectual history, thus, gained in popularity although in this process it lost its coherence. Simultaneously, the range of intellectual history also expanded on account of the humanistic approach in the writings of the literary people, sponsoring the American Studies Movement. However, it should be admitted that much of the work resulting from this inter-disciplinary approach was predominantly literary to qualify as historical. Moreover, literary writers of intellectual history sacrificed wholeness for the sake of expressive power.

To sum up, one may entirely agree with the witty observation that the literary scholars made intellectual history functional to art, as professional historians made it functional to action; and like a lady of easy virtue, it slept wherever it had shelter.

NOTES

1. John Higham, in *Approaches to the Study of the United States*, ed. Henring Cohen, XII, 2, p. 2.
2. James Harvey Robinson, *The New History: Essays Illustrating the Modern Historian Outlook* (New York: Macmillan, 1912).
3. Richard Hofstadter, *Social Darwinism in American Political Thought* (Philadelphia: University of Pennsylvania Press, 1944).
4. Higham, p. 355.

Hindu Influence on Henry David Thoreau

UMESH PATRI

Coming to Thoreau's scriptures one finds that he had no knowledge of Indian scriptures during his college days. Though there were one or two references to the East, such as to Persian writing and Confucius in the essays which he wrote during his Harvard days, his real interest in the East, especially India, started after he came to stay with Emerson. Both Franklin Benjamin Sanborn, the biographer of the Transcendentalists and Bartholow V. Crawford agree that Thoreau had no knowledge of India during his college days and the years that followed immediately. It was Emerson who aroused in him a true enthusiasm for India. Emerson and Thoreau came to know each other in 1837 and Emerson who was at that time immersed in his study of Indian scriptures drew Thoreau's attention to them. Four years later when Thoreau came to stay with Emerson and had an access to his splendid library he began to read some important Indian scriptures like the *Laws of Manu*, the *Bhagavad Gita* and the *Upanisads* which he called the "bibles of India." His journal entries after 1841 bear strong evidence of his attraction to Indian scriptures and his wide reading of them. Two other periods during which he had an opportunity to read Indian scriptures are: years from 1849 to 1854 when he borrowed a large number of Indian scriptures from the Harvard University library and the year 1855 when his English friend Thomas Cholmondeley sent him a gift of forty-four oriental books which contained such titles as the *Rig Veda Samhita*, the *Mandukya Upanisada*, the *Vishnu Purana*, the *Institutes of Manu*, the *Bhagavad Gita* and the *Bhagavata Purana* etc. Some of the important books he borrowed from the Harvard University library were the *Mahabharat*, *Harwansa*, the *Sankhya Karika*, the *Samved Samhita*, the *Sacontala*, or the *Fatal Ring* and the *Bhagavad Gita* etc. William Bysshe Stein has prepared a scholarly bibliography of Hindu and Buddhist texts which Thoreau had read till 1854. The list contains seventy-one titles with an impressive selection of books containing many branches of Indian scriptures and literature such as the *Vedas*, the epics and *Purana*, the *Kavyas*, the story literature

(*Katha*), the dramas, grammar, the *Dharmasastras* and *Smrtis,* philosophy and religion, Buddhist and other vernacular texts.[1]

Thoreau was introduced to Indian scriptures by reading the *Laws of Manu* or *Manu Samhita* as it is known in India. It profoundly impressed his mind and guided him for his future course of action. Immediately after reading the book in 1841 he made an entry in his journal: "The impression which those sublime sentences made on me last night has awakened me before any cockcrowing."[2] He has recorded his impression of this book extensively and in many contexts. The book has impressed on him the doctrine of detachment, renouncement and the need for solitude for a seeker of truth. The following passages taken from Thoreau's various writings suggest his admiration for the *Laws of Manu:*

> I know of no book which comes to us with grander pretensions than the "Laws of Manu"; and this immense presumption is so impersonal and sincere that it is never offensive or ridiculous. Observe the modes in which modern literature is advertised, and then consider this Hindoo prospectus. Think what a reading public it addresses, what criticism it expects. What wonder if the times were not ripe for it?[3]
>
> The "Laws of Manu" are a manual of private devotion, so private and domestic and yet so public and universal a word as is not spoken in the parlor or pulpit in these days. It is so impersonal that it exercises our sincerity more than any other. It goes with us into the yard and into the chamber, and is yet later spoken than the advice of our mother and sisters.[4]
>
> The sublime sentences of Manu carry us back to a time when purification and sacrifice and self-devotion had a place in the faith of men, and were not as now a superstition. They contain a subtle and refined phiosophy also, such as in these times is not accompanied with so lofty and pure a devotion.[5]

The *Vedas* also impressed him in the like manner:

> What extracts from the Vedas I have read fall on me like the light of a higher and purer luminacy, which describes a loftier course through a purer-stratum, free from particulars, simple, universal. It rises on me like the full moon after the stars have come out, wading through some far summer stratum of the sky. . . . The Vedas contain a sensible account of God. The religion and philosophy of the Hebrews are those of a wilder and ruder tribe, wanting the civility and intellectual refinements and subtlety of the Hindoos.

> Man flows at once to God as soon as the channel of purity, physical, intellectual and moral is open.[6]
>
> The veneration in which the Vedas are held is itself a remarkable fact. Their code embraced the whole moral life of the Hindoo, and in such a case there is no other truth than sincerity. Truth is such by reference to the heart of man within, not to any standard without.[7]

In an article on Emerson, I have shown how the *Bhagavad Gita* had greatly influenced and shaped the philosophy of Emerson. Its impact on Thoreau was no less, although the nature of that impact was different. Thoreau read the *Bhagavad Gita* in 1845[8] after reading the *Laws of Manu*. For him *Bhagavad Gita* was much greater thing than "all the ruins of the East!"[9] What appealed to Thoreau in the *Bhagavad Gita* was the philosophy of *niskama karma* or action without attachment and he learnt from it how to give up one's desire. His books like *A Week* and *Walden* and his *Journals* are full of Vedic statements and paraphrased ideas from the *Gita* regarding detachment. He also published a number of fine abstracts from various Hindu scriptures in the various issues of the *Dial*. In *Walden* he writes: "I bathe my intellect in the stupendous and cosmogonal philosophy of the Bhagavat Gita"[10] and in recommending the *Bhagavad Gita* to the American reading public he writes in *A Week:* "I would say to the readers of the Scriptures, if they wish for a good book, read the Bhagavat Geeta, an episode to the Mahabharat . . . translated by Charles Wilkins. It deserves to be read with reverence even by Yankees, as a part of the sacred writings of a devout people, and the intelligent Hebrew will rejoice to find in it a moral grandeur and sublimity akin to those of his own Scriptures."[11]

Thoreau, like other Transcendentalists, had a breadth and catholicity of mind which brought him to the study of religions of the Orient. From the beginning he was disillusioned with the organized Christianity (he never went to the Church) and like Emerson he showed great interest in Hinduism and its philosophy. He confessed his lack of knowledge of Hebraism and his love for Eastern scriptures in *A Week:* "The reading which I love best is the scriptures of the several nations, though it happens that I am better acquainted with those of the Hindoos, the Chinese, and the Persians, than of the Hebrews."[12] The serenity and contemplative nature of Hinduism appealed to him most. In comparison to Hebraism which had originated Christianity, Thoreau found Hinduism superior in many ways. The following passage demonstrates Thoreau's disenchantment with Hebraism and his love for Hinduism:

> The Hindoos are more serenely and thoughtfully religious than the Hebrews. They have perhaps a purer, more independent and impersonal knowledge of God. Their religious books describe the first inquisitive and contemplative access to God, the Hebrews bible a conscientious return, a grosser and more personal repentance. Repentance is not a free and fair highway to God. A wise man will dispense with repentance. It is shocking and passionate. God prefers that you approach him thoughtful, not penitent, though you are the chief of sinners. It is only by forgetting yourself that you draw near to him. The calmness and gentleness with which the Hindoo philosophers approach and discourse on forbidden themes is admirable.[13]

The Christian and Hindu concept of man, Thoreau thinks, are diametrically opposed to each other, the former sees man as a born sinner whereas the latter takes him to be potentially divine. The lofty concept of man embodied in Hinduism had a special appeal to Thoreau's mind. Praising such a concept he writes: "In the Hindoo scripture the idea of man is quite illimitable and sublime. There is nowhere a loftier conception of his destiny. He is at length lost in Brahma himself. The divine male. Indeed, the distinction of races in this life is only the commencement of a series of degrees which ends in Brahma.[14]

The influence of Hinduism had a different effect on Thoreau from that on Emerson. Emerson, as we have seen earlier, took the intellectual and philosophical concepts such as the concepts of Over-Soul, *Maya*, Law of *Karma* and rebirth etc. as refreshing concepts which expanded his vision of life but Thoreau took the Hindu ideals of spiritual life and applied them to his own life. The practical ideals such as renunciation, detachment, need for solitude etc. owned precedence in his mind over the abstract and speculative ideas mentioned above. As Carl T. Jackson says: "Thoreau's response was more general and less intellectual. . . . The concept of an all-embracing God-head or of a self-punishing justice, which won Emerson's intellectual appreciation were largely lost on his younger friend."[15] It may be made clear that though the abstract concepts were lost on Thoreau on the intellectual level they saturated his whole life, making the impact more radical. While in Emerson it remained on the level of belief and intellect, in Thoreau it was translated into daily action. My purpose is to show that in certain ways Thoreau went a step beyond his mentor and in certain other ways complemented him. The influence of India on Thoreau was complex and not so straightforward as it was on Emerson. Hence by mere comparing the passages from Thoreau containing from Hinduism with the passages from the Hindu scriptures having parallel ideas will not be enough. The impact of Hindu scriptures has not only changed Thoreau's thought and vision, but has also directed his life's activities by orienting him to a way of life which is typically Indian. It has resulted in the building of a character which is un-American in many ways and which is closer to a detached Hindu Yogi. So to understand Thoreau one has to study both his life and his writings.

Those who have tried to assess the nature of the Indian influence on Thoreau have come to the conclusion that Thoreau, more than Emerson came closely to follow the Indian doctrines of liberation and translated them into action in his own life in the same way the Indian Yogis did. Critics like Arthur Christy, Frank Macshane and William Bysshe Stein have seen Thoreau as a Yogi. William Bysshe Stein in his two articles, "Thoreau's First Book: A Spoor of Yoga"[16] and "Thoreau's *A Week* and *Om* Cosmography"[17] shows similarity between soul's journey to eternity (the metaphor being that of a river merging into the sea) and Thoreau's symbolic journey in *A Week.* The route that *Jivatman* or individual soul takes to reach the *Paramatman* or Universal Soul, Stein argues, has a symbolic correspondence with the structure of *A Week.* Stein juxtaposes passages from the *Brahman Sutras* and *Yoga Sutras* with those from *A Week* to demonstrate the correspondence.

A Week on Concord and Merrimack Rivers offers a nineteenth century version of the Hindu itinerary of the divine journey (devayana) to spiritual liberation. A symbolic account of Thoreau's gradual mastery of Yoga, the work evinces his disdain of all empirical knowledge, though particularly of Western historicism and its assumption of evolutionary progress. His familiarity with the various modalities of the quest for self-enlightenment is not a matter of speculation. In his *Journal*, essays, and two completed books he constantly quoted from the Hindu religious writings devoted to the elucidation of the subject. However, his execution of *A Week* indicates that he also considers the doctrines of Buddhism as affirmations of the validity of the undertaking."[18]

Stein divides Thoreau's journey into four stages: waking dream (Saturday, Sunday, Monday); waking sleep (Tuesday, Wednesday); in dreams awake (Wednesday, Thursday) and awaking of the true self (Friday). In another article "The Hindu Matrix of *Walden*: The King's Son" [19] he further elucidates the nature and extent of the Indian influence on Thoreau. Frank MacShane's article "*Walden* and Yoga,"[20] like Stein's discusses *Walden* in the light of Yoga. MacShane writes: "Certainly there is no doubt that the book is permeated with a vaguely Hindu atmosphere. There are many overt references to the sacred texts of India. . . . And Thoreau himself follows certain Hindu customs. . . . There are also many less obvious references as for example to the language of silence which is so common in India and which is involved in Thoreau's silent communion with the old fisherman who joined him at the pond."[21] The influence of Hinduism, MacShane seems to suggest, made Thoreau a Yogi. Thoreau himself said in a letter to HGO Blake in 1849 his concept of a Yogi:

> Free in this world as the birds in the air, disengaged from every kind of chains, those who have practised the *yoga* gather in Brahma the certain fruit of their works.
>
> Depend upon it that, rude and careless as I am, I would fain practice the *yoga* faithfully. This yogi, absorbed in contemplation, contributes in his degree to creation, he breathes a divine perfume, he hears wonderful things. Divine forms traverse him without tearing him, and, united to the nature which is proper to him, he goes, he acts as animating original matter.
>
> To some extent, and at rare intervals, even I am a yogi.[22]

While Stein studies Thoreau as a *Jnana Yogin*, MacShane studies him as a *Karma Yogin.* Thoreau was also a *Raja Yogin*, an idea which critics have not touched upon. In fact, what I am going to do in the following pages is to study him as a composite Yogi who on different levels has emphasized different aspects of Yoga, such as *Jnana* (knowledge), *Karma* (action) and spiritual discipline in the line of *astanga yoga* (eight-fold method) of Patanjali. Thoreau's expansion of consciousness through knowledge earns him the title of *Jnana Yogi*, and his following of the principles of detached action and his *phalatrushna vairagya* or renunciation of the fruit of action make him a *karma yogin.* His lifestyle characterized by *tapasya* (austerities), his hatred of materialism, commercialism and industrialism (*Vishaya ninda*); his life of poverty, his love of solitude, his *vairagya* or asceticism, his practice of *ahimsa* and vegetarianism, his yogi state of contentment, his description of his own trancelike states (akin to samadhi), his intuitional grasp of the music of the universe akin to the mystical sound of *OM* (or *AUM*); his withdrawal from society and acceptance of fate; his lack of worldly ambition in life all these bring him very close to the Hindu ascetic.

NOTES

1. William Bysshe Stein, "A Bibliography of Hindu and Buddhist

Literature Available to Thoreau through 1854," *ESO*, no. 47, part 2 (II Qtr., 1967), pp. 52-56.

2. Henry David Thoreau, *Writings*, ed. Bradfird Torrey (New York: Ams Press, 1986), VII, 267. (*Journal*, Aug. 7, 1941).
3. *Ibid*., p. 264. (*Journal*, I, June 7, 1841).
4. *Ibid*., p. 279. (*Journal*, I, Sept. 1, 1841).
5. *Ibid*., p. 280. (*Journal*, I, Sept. 2, 1841).
6. *Ibid*., VIII, p. 4. (*Journal*, II, 1850).
7. *Ibid*.,VII, pp. 275-76. (*Journal*, I, Aug. 28, 1841).
8. See John T. Reid, *Indian Influence in American Literature and Thought* (New Delhi: Indian Council for Cultural Relations, 1965), p.35.
9. Thoreau, *Writings*, X, p. 153. (*Journal*, IV, June 25, 1852).
10. *Ibid*., II, p. 328. (*Walden*).
11. *Ibid*., I, pp. 147-48. (*A Week*).
12. *Ibid*., p. 72.
13. *Ibid*., VIII, p. 3. (*Journal*, II, 1850).
14. *Ibid*., VII, p. 275. (*Journal*, I, Aug. 28, 1841).
15. Carl T. Jackson, "Oriental Ideas in American Thought," *Dictionary of the History of Ideas*, ed. Philip P.Wiener ((New York: Charles Scribner's, 1973), III, p. 431.
16. *ESO*, no. 41 (IV Qtr., 1965), pp. 4-25.
17. *Artist and Citizen Thoreau*, ed. John J. McAleer (Hartford: Transcendental Books, 1971), pp. 15-37.
18. *Ibid*., p. 15.
19. Stein, "The Hindu Matrix of *Walden*: Thè King's Don," *Comparative Literature*, XXII, 3 (Summer 1970), pp. 303-18.
20. Frank MacShane, "Walden and Yoga," *The New England Quarterly*, XXXVII, 3 (Sept. 1964), pp. 322-42.
21. *Ibid*, pp. 322-23.
22. Thoreau, *Writings*, VI, p. 175.

The Role of Indian Women Immigrants in the US

VIRBALA BRAHMABHATT

In the present century various attempts have been made for the emancipation of women. The role of women in today's world is becoming important. But there are very few studies of Indian women immigrants in the US. In this context it would be interesting and informative to investigate the role of Indian women immigrants in the American society. In this paper I have attempted to show the role played by Indian women immigrants in the first decade of the twentieth century.

A handful of Indians came to the US in the nineteenth century, but we are not sure about the number of female immigrants to the US at that particular period of time. We have an account about the first lady Anandibai Joshi who came to America in 1883 for her studies in Medicine. She was hardly seventeen-years-old when she reached this source of the US. We have instance of this Indian woman, who followed most traditional Indian way of life in the American system. Mrs. Carpenter was a constant source of comfort. Anandibai spent four months with the Carpenter family in the beginning. She used to narrate stories from the *Ramayana* and the *Mahabharata* to Carpenter's children and offered her friends pure Indian food. Thus she tried to maintain her Indian culture in American society.[1]

In the autumn of the same year Anandibai started her studies. The dean of her women's Medical College of Philadelphia was Miss Bodley who very much appreciated a girl from India in the face of all opposition from the society and the poverty in which she was born for the sake of acquiring medical knowledge. She therefore offered her a grant of $ 600 for three years. It is also significant to note that this dean had arranged a meeting to welcome Anandibai and also arranged for a room for her quite near the college. It was the first time that an Indian woman had come all the way to America to be educated. Anandibai fulfilled her dream of becoming a doctor in the US. She also stood first in her class despite several handicaps. It was then her desire to work for women in India. So she returned but did not live long.

Another woman Pandita Ramabai visited America in response to an invitation from her cousin Anandibai. The Pandita's idea to open a home of study for young widows in India found a number of adherents, and eventually Ramabai Association was formed, which guaranteed the finance of High Caste Widow's Home in India for ten years. She returned to India is 1889.[2] In 1890 Rakhambai, a Maharashtrian woman came to the USA for her studies in Medicine. She returned to India in 1894 and became the first professional doctor in Marathi community.[3]

In the first decade of the twentieth century women from India started coming to the US but they remained essentially as housewives. It is significant to know that the first Indian woman immigrant who enrolled herself as a student was Padma Chandra in 1974 at University of California. Another example of a woman who applied for citizenship of the US was in 1916 and her name was Kanta Gupta.

Even a casual survey of women coming to the US from India indicate that most of them came as housewives some portion of them later on started working to supplement the income of the family. Very few of them studied in the US and secured employments as professional as well as in the universities.

The first Indian settlers in America were mainly Sikh peasant farmers pushed out of Canada who ended up in California in the early 1900s. A few students along with some political refugees, arrived in the US In 1907, 1072 and in 1908, 1710 Indians entered the US and the number increased[4] thereafter.[5] Indian immigrants entering the US between 1870 to 1965:

Year	Immigrants
1871-1880	163
1881-1890	269
1891-1900	68
1901-1910	4713
1911-1920	2082
1921-1930	1886
1931-1940	496
1941-1950	1761
1951-1960	1973
1961-1965	2602
Total	16013

(US Immigration Service Annual Report, Washington DC Government Printing Office, 1975, 62-64)

People of Indian origin come to the US not only from India but also from the countries of East Africa the West Indies, Guyana and Europe (Great Britain in particular) but most of them directly come from India. In 1909 Immigration Commission survey in California of 474 male 'Hindoo' farm workers found that 215 were married but wives of all of them had remained in India. (One such young husband, nurturing memories of his teenage bride, was not able to send for her for forty years. As she got off the plane in San Francisco, in bewilderment he gasped, "But she is such an old woman.") The wives left behind in Punjab poured out their sorrows and frustration in songs. In 1910 one woman and two girls arrived in San Francisco from India bringing the total number of Indian women on the West Coast to six.

Sikhs had migrated to Bellingham in Washington, to work in the lumber trade. They were resented by other West Coast labourers because of their willingness to work for law wages and rival lumbermen soon forced them to shift farther south to the rich farming areas of the Sacramento, San Jaoguin and Imperial Valleys. Their number however was small. Only 7000 entered between 1904 and 1923 including only 30 females.[8]

In 1917 Immigration Act established 'Barred Zones' to prohibit immigration of labourers from virtually all Asian countries except Japan. Consequently between 1923 and 1926 the US government cancelled the naturalization certificates of 60 Indian Americans. Some American women married to them also lost their citizenship. Taraknath Das became a citizen around 1913. He married an American woman.[9] Because of this reason many Indian men married Mexican women because such marriages were permitted by the US law since the Mexican women were eligible for citizenship. The children born of such marriages became American citizens.

In the decades that followed many unsuccessful attempts were made to correct the situation. However nothing much was achieved till II World War. President Torluman came out in support of the Indian quota bill and finally on 2nd July 1946 signed the Act making Indians eligible for US citizenship and providing for an immigration quota of 100 per annum for the country. After II World War scholarships and exchange programs stimulated Indian students to pursue higher education in American universities. But the flow of immigrants was very slow. Many of the earlier immigrants were largely uneducated and often unskilled. But in contrast after 1965 Immigration laws raised the quota of aliens and permitted entry to twenty thousand educated people from each Asian country. Indian immigrants represent one of the most highly educated ethnic groups ever to come to this country. The immigrating Indians, because the Act of 1965 favoured people with technical skills, have usually been highly educated and for the most part have succeeded well in the American economy. Several surveys carried out in urban areas of the US indicated that three fourths of Indian male immigrants were college graduates.

More recently, less educated Indian immigrants are coming under categories of family unification rather than, meeting the technical expertise critieria.[10]

1965	582
1966	2,458
1967	2,642
1968	4,682
1969	5,963
1970	10,114
1971	14,310
1972	16,926
1973	12,256
1974	11,863
1975	14,939
Total	96,735

At present, since the immigration laws give priority to blood relations of American citizens, their sisters, brothers and parents receive preference over doctors, engineers, scientists and other professionals on the waiting lists. By 1980 it rose to 361531 and in 1990 815447.[11] Approximately 1,00,000 were living in metropolitan New York, 58,800 in California and remainder widely dispersed across the country. Some were spread through the south west where 'Patel Motels' became common.[12]

In the first phase of immigrants we find that the women were housewives accompanying their husbands to look after the household and the children. Nand Kaur came to the US in 1920 with her husband and she used to look after her seven children at home in Yuba city of California.[13] But gradually we find a competitive atmosphere and clash of egos between the labour class women and the professionally qualified women. After 1965 many of early Indian immigrant women came from relatively wealthy land and business-owning families from India but after coming to

USA wives of immigrant labourers often lived difficult and impoverished lives. Another reason was those women came from elite families especially Brahmin and Kshatriya origin they were not supposed to work since their husbands were well off in USA. But the women immigrants after 1976 gave a completely different picture. We find them coming from a cross-section of society and not financially well off. Because of this reason the family in US after 1970 reflects changes in population and the economy. The family size was smaller, there were greater female participation in the labour force and other works. Women were affected by the double burden of domestic work and outside work in different ways depending upon their particular circumstances.

In the US we find a number of Indian women who work outside the home as compared to their traditional role in India. Indian families seemed to have adopted the practice of husband and wife working. About 40% of Indian immigrant women are employed full time, 10% occasionally and 7% part time.[14]

For the young bride, adjustment was also difficult. She was brought to the new country by a man who regularly left for work at 6 a.m. and did not return until 6 or 7 p.m. Being used to gregariousness of joint family living, she became lonely and depressed. When she had children she felt overworked and burdened because there were no servants to help and take care of the house and baby.

The elderly women were usually unhappy in the US. They had no friends or status in America. They were left alone all day with nothing to do except watch TV. They got bored and yet they often did not feel confident enough to mix with the Americans. They could not tolerate the severe winter months.

In general the dress, speech and mannerisms of Indian children in the US resemble those of other American young people. However conflicts arose because along with preserving their traditional Indian language, food, entertainment and religion. Indian parents had other norms which they wanted their children to keep. They definitely wanted their children to have arranged marriage preferably with a spouse from India.

After World War II we find women from an economically low background taking any jobs available to them since they were not skilled labourers and not able to communicate fluently in English. The vast majority of Punjabi Sikh men who work in the cannery were middle-aged, most of them work in the lower paying jobs. Not only was work in cannery monotonous it was also uncomfortable and sometimes dangerous.[15] But in spite of all these shortcomings they continued to work in the canneries to provide more income to their families while fulfilling their domestic roles as wives and mothers. Those women were satisfied with working at the cannery which was better than doing farmwork. By this work they contributed to their families' income.

Indian newcomers often see the opportunity to strike it rich though entrepreneurship is the most attractive option they have. Many of the businesses are food stores, Indian Grocery stores, Sari stores, eating or drinking establishment and Motel or Hotel business. Winnick quotes Thomas Muller, an authority on immigration, on the Indians' ubiquitous hold on the motel industry. 1982 Indians owned over 3100 hotels and motels across the land, ten percent of all such establishments in the nation. Previous owners were simply unwilling to devote the long hours and hard work necessary to remain in business. Motels are considered good investment by Indians because the family can be utilized to run these establishments.[16] Generally a wife runs the business while the husband works elsewhere at a salaried job. These low budget hotels and motels encompass a wide range of work such as room cleaning, laundry, phone reception, counter work seven days a week, twenty four hours a day. Mrs. Patel describes her typical day: "I get up at 5.30 in the morning, make breakfast for the family, get the two children ready for school. If there is a guest, I check him in. After the kids are gone, I clean the rooms which have just been vacated, and make all the beds, take out the laundry. In the evening the guests start coming and check them in. Then I cook."[17] Generally women in grocery stores help their husbands. They work 7 a.m. to 7 p.m., six and a half days a week with no time off.

In the 1960s and 1970s Indian girls were crazy to go to the US. Some of them were from very high and aristocratic families and still they got married to boys of greencardholders from the US coming essentially from low families. There are instances these girls asked for divorce after some years because they could not live happily with boys having low cultural background.

Semi-educated women married greencardholders. They became computer programmers, beauticians, teachers, dental assistants and sales girls in the US. Most of the people who went to England remained conservative because they were from African territories, they were not directly from India. The conservative atmosphere in England also did not give them scare from liberalized lifestyle. But in the US women came directly from India and the liberal atmosphere in the US also helped them in observing progressive and modern view. Even more recent immigrant women from middle-class white collar backgrounds frequently find work in semi-skilled jobs. Their consciousness and aspirations nevertheless remain middle-class.

Educated women from India living in the US showed that 33.8 percent of the women working in technical field and 50 percent in academic field described themselves as feminists.[18]

Popularly known as America Born Confused Desis (ABCDS) many Indian children brought up in the US confront the familiar dilemma of being torn between two cultures. Trying to adopt socially but looking foreign, burdened by the contradictory expectation of their Indian parents and American peers, uncertain of which heritage to claim as their own and without a sense of belonging, they seem destined to be misfits in both cultures, for them youth is often a time of crisis.[19] This problem is very acute for the girls who are born and brought up there. First generation of immigrant parents prefer to have their daughters married in traditional arranged marriages. This practice is reflected in the increased number of matrimonial advertisements in the past decade in immigrant newspapers such as 'India Abroad.'

Indian-Americans attempt to preserve their Indianness through many organizations such as temple societies, regional cultural groups and other religious groups which have proliferated wherever Indians live in this country. More than 500 Indian associations are scattered throughout the state.[20] Fisher's study of New York Indians uncovered 44 Indian organisations in the New York area. In 1913 Taraknath Das established a small foundation to help Indian students abroad.[21] It was the beginning of the establishment of Indian organisations in USA. In 1960 the Association of Indians in America (AIA) was unique among the formally chartered Indian groups in USA. After this many Associations were established.[22] Although there are numerous associations, they are largely cultural or religious in their concerns and trend, not to address issues of socio-political significance. Even where such issues are beginning to be addressed there has been a noticeable lack of attention to the particular concerns of women immigrants from the Indian subcontinent. However, over the past decade a number of women recognizing the need for a separate forum for articulating their unique concerns have formed autonomous grassroot organizations in different parts of America and Canada. More than dozen of these groups have sprung up, founded by and composed entirely of women. These groups highlight the experience, concerns and contributions of women from the Indian subcontinent.

Let us look at some of the associations concerned with Indian women immigrants. First one is Manvi. It is concerned with issues and problems faced by Asian Indian women in USA, to work towards social change and create visible ethnic identity for Asian Indian women, support women's struggle for equality in India and other countries. It organized self-protection seminars in the wake of racial violence against Indian community. It helps displaced home makers and victims of domestic abuse. It established with other groups a legal defence fund for women in financial need. Manavi Newsletter is published by Manvi, three times a year.[23] Sakhi is another association established in New York concerned with domestic violence within South Asian women in New York. To support and empower battered women, they give legal advice. It has a resource centre.[24] The New York based-Association of Asian Indian women in America took part in a White House briefing on Asian American women. The committee on South Asian women has published a monograph containing a bibliography on women's status, a statistical over-view and a directory of organizations and individuals committed to improving the status of women in South Asia. In addition the group produces an internationally circulated quarterly publication, the COSAW Bulletin, which features theme-oriented articles, essays, interviews, book reviews, research index and reports on the activities of other South Asian women's groups.[25]

Though we don't have enough evidence of the contribution of women in various fields prior to the 1960s, we have the following illustrious examples of few women who have substantially contributed to American life and culture. Famous Gujarati poet Panna Nayak, for instance, is a senior Librarian in a University in USA. She is one of such early migrants. Her book of poems, *Philadelphia* is a text book in an undergraduate course in the SNDT University for women in Bombay. Bharati Mukherjee, an Indian American immigrant author, is gaining increasing recognition in the US. Her two novels, *The Tiger's Daughter* (1971) and *Wife* (1975), and her short story collection *Darkness* (1985) have earned her high praise from critics here as well as prestigious prizes, fellowships and awards.[26] Bharati Mukherjee and Ved Mehta are among the more prominent Asian authors who have won critical acclaim. Sucheta Mazumdar and Pratibha Parmar, Jyotsna Vaid, Meena Alexander, Rashmi Luthra are eminent writers and have presented papers in various forums in the US. Indian singers, instrumentalists and dancers have a tremendous impact on American society. Many America-born Indian girls are learning Bharatnatayam, Kathak, etc. in dancing schools. At 22 Priya Mayadas Sable is an accomplished concert pianist and composer. Her parents immigrated to the US in 1975, where Priya studied at various music schools. She has won numerous awards.[27]

In politics also women are taking interest. Kanak Datta, an Asian Indian woman, ran for a seat in the New Jersey Legislative Assembly in 1981. Though she lost election, she did well in the returns and may run again.[28]

An attempt has been made in this paper to discuss the contribution of women immigrants in detail. This is a topic which needs more research because many resources remain to be tapped. Indian women's role as teachers and professionals working in the US needs to be explored further.

NOTES

1. S.J. Joshi, *Anandi Gopal*, trans. from Marathi (Calcutta, 1992), p. 219.
2. Padmini Sen Gupta, *Pioneer Women of India* (Bombay, 1944), p. 10.
3. *Vaibhav*, 11 Dec. 1894.
4. Ramesh Babu, "The Indian American: A Minority in the Making" in *Minorities and the American Political System* (Delhi, 1989) p. 136.
5. Fisher P. Maxine, *The Indians of New York City—A Study of Immigrants from India* (New York, 1980) p. 11.
6. Sucheta Mazumdar, "A Woman Centered Perspective on Asian American History," *Making Waves*, An anthology of writings by and about Asian American Women, p. 5.
7. Judy Youg, "A Chronology of Asian American History," *Ibid*., p. 425.
8. Arthur and Usha Helweg, "Indians in America Doing Well," quoted in *Span*, February 1982, p. 15.
9. Leonard A. Gordon, "The Indian Experience," quoted in *Span*, January 1992, p.18.
10. Fisher P. Maxine, p. 12.
11. Richard L Worsnop, "Asian American," quoted in *Congressional Quarterly Researcher*, December 13, 1991, p. 948.
12. *Span*, 1982, p. 17.
13. *Span*, 1992, p. 21.
14. B. Donald Johnson, "Asians Growing up in America: Case Studies from New York," presented at Cornell University, April 15, 1989.
15. William Marcelle, "Ladies on the Line: Punjabi Cannery Workers in Central California" in *Making Waves* p. 155.
16. Lious Winnick, "Model Minority," *Span*, Jan. 1992, p. 19.
17. Sucheta Mazumdar, p. 18.
18. *Ibid*., p. 16.
19. "America Born Confused Desis," *India Today*, 31 August 1989.
20. *Span*, 1982.
21. *Span*, 1992.
22. Fisher P. Maxine, p. 109.
23. Subhadra Patwa, *Directory of Women's Organization (India &*

Abroad) (Bombay, 1985), p. 161.
24. *Ibid*., p. 165.
25. Jyotsna Vaid, "Seeking a Voice – South Asian Women's Groups in North America," *Making Waves*, p. 401.
26. "Bharati Mukherji," *Span*, June 1990, p. 32.
27. Savitri Makhijani, "Young Pianist," quoted in *Span*, June 1992, p. 11.
28. Judy Chu, "Asian Pacific American Women in Mainstream Politics," *Making Waves*, p. 410.

A Case for Presidential Government in India

P. M. KAMATH

American studies in India had a chequered growth during the last forty five years as Indo-US relations constantly came under the clouds caused by the stresses and strains of International cold war. As a result, Indian funding agencies have done very little to promote American studies in a systematic way, leaving it mainly to the American funding agencies or the binational agencies like the USEFI and the ASRC. However, Indian policymakers have not thought it necessary to do their own bit to promote American studies. A facile reason sometimes offered for American studies not being considered as an area study is that it does not require study of a foreign language. Thus, India and America are separated by so to say common language – English.

Hence, outside the JNU, I doubt whether there is any university in India which has a full-fledged centre for study of America. In University of Bombay, for instance, American studies was sought to be introduced in the early 1960s with the help of University of Pennsylvania. But the conventional departmental boundaries were so strong that readers recruited to study America got scattered amongst the departments of history, politics and literature rather than remain as one unit. But since then one person specializing on America in each Department has not even grown into two – contrary to Parkinson's law. This is in contrast to study of the erstwhile Soviet Union. What the Indian Americanists have often encountered, instead, is a charge of being a CIA agent!

However, whenever any discussion has taken place on the question of increasing contacts between the Indian scholars and their American counterparts, obviously on the American initiative, our educational bureaucrats have not hesitated to plead that they too be included in the academic exchange programme!

Be that as it may, I have always tried to find answers to the question. Why study the US – be its politics or history or literature or culture or civilization? There are many reasons which could be advanced to answer the question. One vital reason is that the US today has emerged as the only veto-wielding major power in the UN with a will-power to commit its superior military strength for the collective good – albeit as it sees it. To learn about the US therefore is to remove our own ignorance, so as to enable us to make our policies more effective in achieving their goals. Such ignorance galore in our general public and policy makers, including law makers. Public ignorance deserves to be eliminated but its impact on our bilateral relations is indirect. But ignorance on the part of policymakers can cause avoidable harm to the friendly relations. To give one example, very few of our policymakers are aware of the fact that fragmented governmental structure in the US cannot always act or speak without cacophony. Thus, in 1983 when a few legislators along with a very low level State Department official met some Sikh separatists outside the committee room, the India MPs created an uproar alleging the US government interference in our internal affairs.

Another reason is that as a developed political system with a continuous history of two hundred and sixteen years, I feel that the US can offer us some insights as to how to organize our ever-evolving political system. This is true of our literature too to some extent. Most of those who have contributed a great deal to creative work in our regional language literature like Marathi or Kannada, have themselves been teachers of English or more specifically American literature. If I do not venture to mention some names of such creative writers, it is for the simple reason that I do not wish to generate a controversy from those who are left out as well as those included.

In the area of comparative political system where I can claim some expertise I wish to submit that we can search for some answers to our own problems, as the American political experience has given to mankind certain unique political concepts to organize sharing of political power like federalism and presidential system. The countries of South Asian region, for instance, look to our democratic political experience to develop their own democratic institutions.

Today, Inida, as an ancient society, attempting to build a modern political system is facing three major challenges. First communalization of politics; second, political instability and third as a consequence of the first two challenges a threat to national unity and integrity. As India has faced many challenges in the past and somehow managed to survive, there is a false complacency that we could overcome present challenges as well. But it is my considered opinion that we are sitting on the tip of a volcano and it might erupt any time if corrective steps are not taken. Hence, before these challenges go out of control, I strongly feel that we need to switch over to a presidential system of government. Tinkering with the existing parliamentary system won't help us any more. Presidential government need not be a copy of the American system. But by borrowing essentials from the American system and applying modifications to suit changed times, our major political problems can be brought under control.

India is a multiregional, multilinguistic, and multireligious society. This diversity and this heterogeneity, our founding fathers tried to hold together in a parliamentary system within a federal structure. This was imitative of the British parliamentary system as introduced by the Government of India Act, 1935. This is unlike the American experience. After their independence from the British colonialism, Americans, though familar with the British parliamentary system, created a unique system of presidential government within a federal structure to hold together their heterogeneous population.

The parliamentary system can function well only when there is a two party system. In a more homogeneous society as in Britain parliamentary system had political instability whenever the Labour Party faced splits as in 1924 and 1929. Basic problem with the parliamentary democracy in India is one of our failure to develop two or three national political parties. With the Indian National Congress inheriting the mantle of glory of freedom struggle, the Congress party enjoyed one party dominance nationally. But by 1967 there were clear signs that All India National Congress was losing its national character and emerging as only vote-catching and power-sharing device. In the process, the Congress developed a pluralistic political majority in different states by putting together dominant castes and minority communities-based coalitions, like (KHAM) Kshatriya, Harijans, Adivasis and Muslims in Gujarat.

The system of appealing for voters,.selecting candidates, appointing men to executive positions on caste and communal basis is the Congress strategy to begin with. This was only vulgarized by V.P. Singh in his effort to develop an alternative to the Congress. He started with MAJGAR – Muslims, Ahirs, Jats, Gujars and Rajputs – coalition and later tried to expand it by adding the OBCs by announcing the acceptance of recommendations of Mandal. The BJP answered it by taking up Mandir-Masjid issue and trying to bring together highly pluralistic Hindus under their political banner. Today, all political parties from the left to the right are basically communal as once asserted by Justice Krishna Iyer.

Why this communalization of political process? It is mainly because, in the parliamentary system an MP who aspires to lead the nation as the Prime Minister must command a sizeable following within the party to be the leader of the legislature party. To do so Indian leaders have found it easy to appeal on caste and communal basis and present themselves as protectors of one or the other section of the community instead of developing issue and programme based parties. In this kind of caste and community based politics, power sharing blatantly comes to be on the same basis as the strength of the caste or community in the parliament. As a result, it is better to be a leader of a small party commanding loyalties on a communal basis than to be a part of issue-based political parties.

When too many parties get elected, forming a stable government becomes difficult and a coalition or a minority government becomes inevitable. But from the caste or communal angle, a cabinet post in a coalition is assured to a caste-oriented party rather than when that particular caste or community follows a national issue-based party. This has tended to fragment Indian political parties. Thus in spite of the Congress and Janata Dal and others wooing Scheduled Castes, they have found it necessary to form their own party—Bahujan Samaj Party in UP as Jats from Western UP have come out from the Janata Dal after it lost the power in 1990. Today, there are 33 political parties or factions in the Lok Sabha while the first Lok Sabha, after 1952 elections had only five political parties.

In the process no political party has been able to get a ruling majority after 1984 elections. So long this trend of appealing for votes and posts on caste and communal basis continues, fragmentation of political parties is bound to continue. The result of communalization of electoral politics has been political instability both at the states and at the centre. Instability in states is not a new phenomenon but political instability at the centre is a new phenomenon particularly under the Congress Party dispensation.

What has brought this change at the centre? Clearly the absence of a ruling family. Mrs. Gandhi and Rajiv Gandhi tried to maintain their individual control over the party and the government, through their iron rule of political destabilization of individual Chief Ministers in the Congress Party-ruled states whenever they showed any proclivity to independent action. Since the end of the Nehru-Gandhi family rule, the centre has seen political instability as well, on a day-to-day basis. It is politics all the way. Hence, the Government has no time to govern. If in the past non-Congress efforts to form the government at the centre have invariably ended in the vertical splits in the ruling party—Janata Party in 1979 and the Janata Dal in 1990, whether the Congress Party can avoid it, is not clear today.

In contrast to this, American presidential system has been able to provide a reasonable degree of political stability. Reasonable, because after constitution imposed a two-term ban on presidential aspirants, after Franklin D. Roosevelt was elected for a fourth term, only two—Eisenhower and Reagan were able to complete 8 years in the office. As against it, seven presidents were in the White House for less than two terms. It still appears reasonable stability when we note that Carter in his four year term, dealt with three Indian Prime Ministers and Bush in four years saw four Indian Prime Ministers. This stability in the American system is based on the principle of separation of powers between the executive and legislative branches which has made President coordinate and independent with Congress in respect of term, powers, functions and constituency. President thus enjoys a fixed tenure and cannot be removed by the Congress except through impeachment which is extremely difficult and rare.

Presidential system in the US has also been able to provide a two party system based on policies, despite the US being as heterogeneous as India is. The explanation for this is in the fact that president is elected by the entire nation as a constituency. He has to appeal to a national electorate. This, he cannot do on the basis of advocacy of group or ethnic or sectional interests. He has to develop his platform on the basis of certain broad national policies to get elected. Any presidential aspirant perceived as appealing on the basis of group or sectional interest, is likely to be defeated. This is evident from the fact that though the Democrats enjoy a majority- following in the country while the Republicans are a political minority, since the end of World War II, Republicans were in the White House for twenty years while the Democrats only for 16 years, until Clinton was elected in 1992, though the Democrats were longer in power in the Congress. One important reason for the defeat of Democrats, particularly Walter Mondale in 1984 and Michael Dukakis in 1988 is public perception of them as trying to subserve group interests rather than national interests.

It is also borne out by the facts that any presidential candidate campaigning on an extremely narrow policy posture is likely to be defeated as shown by the defeat of Republican, Bary Goldwater in 1964 and Democrat, George McGovern in 1972. Ronald Reagan, on the other hand, though began with an extreme right wing platform, as the elections approached nearer, moved to the centre of the political fulcrum. This of course, has made two political parties – Republican and Democrats being pragmatic and broad based – often look alike.

Thus it may be reiterated that the Americans, though as heterogeneous as we in India are, have been able to develop a two party system based on policies and programmes than sheer ethnic calculations. American political scientists are of the opinion that a two party system in a multiethnic, multiracial and multilinguistic society is the gift of presidential system. As Professor Arthur MacMahan says that the "influence of the presidential office more than any other factor discouraged the development of the multiplicity of parties."

This phenomenon is the result of the fact that any presidential contest between more than two or three serious candidates in American winner-take-all system is likely to throw the election into the House of Representatives. That is the procedure to be followed if no candidate gets an absolute majority of the electoral college votes. Political parties prefer to avoid the uncertainty of presidential election through the House in which each state has a single vote, determined through a vote of state's representatives.

The presidential system in India need to include a provision that a presidential candidate ought to get fifty percent plus one vote in the notional election. If too many run, here should be a runoff election. The experience of run-off election and uncertainty underlying it, would certainly make different political forces in the country to form some sort of loose coalitions as national political parties. Such national parties cannot be developed on the basis of caste and communal calculations without any reference to policies and programme to make a party platform nationally acceptable.

Another cause of political instability in the Indian parliamentary system is the notorious game of political defections. The buying and selling of MPs is so well known that it was said that Rs. 50 lakhs was a median sum offered to an MP to defect from the Janata Dal of VP Singh in early November 1990.

In a presidential system, the elected members are free to defect on legislation from their own party on certain specific programmes advocated by the president. Occasionally such defection may be on consideration other than policy preferences of a legislator. But his defection does not bring down the government as in a parliamentary system as it happened in India in 1979 or 1990. As a matter of fact a threat of, or actual defection of legislators helps to secure greater responsiveness of the president to Congress as a threat defection in a parliamentary system. But in a parlimentary system such defections invariably introduce a period of political instability leading to erosion of the democratic credibility of the Government. Presidential system avoids that kind of situation. Hence the independence of term that the American Congress enjoys has made it the most powerful democratic legislature in the world. It can discuss, deliberate, differ or defer or even destroy President's legislative measures without any fear of prospect of another electoral uncertainty through a fresh election.

Now let me turn to the third challenge of threat to the national unity and integrity of India. What is the systemic factor contributing to it? In addition to the two challenges of communalization of politics and political instability, highly centralized federal structure acts as a factor. In my opinion some of our problems of secessionism in Punjab or Kashmir have their origin in the feeling or peripheralization among the people of these states. Under presidential system, the federal structure will work well and also federalize the party system. As at the federal level, we will have a directly-elected governor heading the State government. This will ensure much-needed political stability in the states as not only he cannot be removed from the office by the state legislature but he cannot also be removed by the Centre. It is also outside the scope of the new system, where the Central High Command of the ruling party can destabilize a state government, whether it is ruled by the party ruling at the centre or not.

A federal polity with a federalized political process can ensure a reasonable political stability at the centre and in states which will go a long-way in enhancing a sense of participatory democracy among the people thereby curbing secessionist tendencies. Despite that if a state threatens to secede, a nationally elected president is better able to handle the situation between the two elections, as shown by the American Civil War experience than the parliamentary system. A Prime Minister has to consider about political fall-out within the cabinet and within the party before ordering drastic steps. He cannot say "seven nays and one aye, and the aye have it," as reportedly stated by Abraham Lincoln.

Critics of presidential system say that unlike in the parliamentary system, executive in presidential system is not accountable to the elected representatives though he is accountable to the people through his direct election. This is a glib observation. Because unless he keeps the elected representatives on his political side, he cannot get his legislative measures approved. He can do so only by being responsive to the wishes of the representatives. For this, he has to care, cajole, compromise and cooperate with the Congress which in effect secures his accountability. Does the accountability to the executive mean only his frequent removability?

Another important criticism is that the presidential system is more prone to dictatorship than the parliamentary one. However parliamentary system is equally prone to the tendency of building a dictatorship as shown by Mrs. Indira Gandhi's emergency rule. Ultimately eternal public vigilance is the price of democracy. And looking at the present dismal political scenario in the country, a ray of hope for India is to emerge as a presidential nation by the 21st century.

In the preparation of this presidential address, I have drawn from the following of my publications:

1. "Politics of defection in India in the 1980s," *Asian Survey* (Berkeley), October 1985.
2. "Antidote for Communalism," *The Indian Post*, January 9, 1990.

3. "Over-centralised politics negates federalism," *The Times of India*, July 18, 1990.
4. "Destabilisation drama," *Mid-day*, February 15, 1991.
5. "Evolving a New Equation," *The Illustrated Weekly of India*, June 1, 1991.
6. "Coalition conundrum," *The Illustrated Weekly of India*, July 13-19, 1991.
7. "For presidency," *Indian Express*, December 14, 1991.
8. "A case for presidential Democracy," *Span*, June 1992.
9. "Conjuring up the magic number," *The Observer of Business and Politics*, October 16, 1992.
10. "Power to a political majority," *The Independent*, December 21, 1992.
11. "Switching over to presidential system," *Free Press*, February 1, 1993.
12. *Indian Politics under Mrs. Gandhi: Reflective Essays* (New Delhi: South Asian Publishers, 1993).

Vietnam in the Presidential Election of 1992

V.Y.D. RAMAN

"An old letter on an emotional issue comes back to haunt a candidate" bemoaned *The New York Times.*[1] Bill Clinton's 23 year old letter addressed to Col. Eugene Holmes, the then Director, Reserve Officers Training Corps (ROTC) at the University of Arkansas, raked up "painful memories of national division over Vietnam" threatening the chances of the Arkansas governor winning the Democratic ticket and, of course, the White House.[2]

The scope of this paper is confined to the valuation of Bill Clinton's role in the draft affair and the extent of American response to the "unmitigated disaster"[3] of the Vietnam war in the 1992 Presidential election.

William Jefferson Clinton, five times governor of the Southern State of Arkansas, was no novice to politics. As a liberal and moderate Democrat, he had endeared himself to the rank and file of the party. Since his rendezvous with President Kennedy in 1963, Clinton had worked out a carefully planned programme for climbing seats of power in the hierarchy till he became the governor of Arkansas at the young age of 32. With his George Town, Oxford (U.K) and Yale education, he acquired practical knowledge and experience with government, international law and practice. His association in Senator Fulbright, Chairman of the Senate Foreign Relations Committee and his intimate association with anti-war leaders had solidified certain convictions in Clinton on Vietnam war.[4]

The election season in USA began in late 1991 with Mario Cuomo, Governor of New York opting out of the Democratic race. Bill Clinton began with a big bang his orchestrated campaign for this party ticket with the assistance of the core group in the Democratic Party—the Democratic Leadership Council (DLC).[5] The DLC's creature the progressive policy Institute (PPI), a Washington think tank did the major work of the election manifesto of the party. By early 1992 Clinton had succeeded in drawing public attention to the woes of the Bush presidency. He blamed the Republicans for the galloping unemployment rate and the unprecedented recession stalking America. The National debt of the

United States, according to Mr. Clinton, rose from $ 734 billions in 1980 when Ronald Reagan assumed office to $ 4 trillion in July 1992 and the budgetary deficit stood at a staggering figure of $ 333 billions in September 1992.[6]

Mr. Clinton succeeded in focussing attention to the broken premises of the Bush administration including Busis "Read my lips, no new taxes and the fallout of the Reago-nomics." (*Span*, Dec. 92, p. 7) Clinton reminded the Ambulans that President Bush failed to create even one million out of a projected thirty million jobs. (*Frontline*, p. 10) In his strident speeches, Mr. Clinton had succeeded in convincing the majority of Americans of the "mess" created by the Republican regime. He sarcastically remarked that 'Four years ago, candidate Bush said America is special place, not just another pleasant country somewhere over the United Nations roll call between Albania and Zimbabwe. Now, under president Bush, America has an unpleasant economy stuck somewhere between Germany and Sri Lanka. And for most Americans, Mr. President, life is a lot less kind and a lot less gentle than it was before your administration took office. I say, George Bush, if you won't use your power to help America, step aside; I will."[7]

Bill Clinton's amazing success in focussing the failures of the Republican regime and the distress of the Americans sent shock waves in Bush's camp. The aura of Desert Storm which gave president Bush 91 percent popular rating had dwindled to 32 percent by Feburary 1992.[8] Alarmed at the "invincibility" of Mr. Clinton's choice his opponents had unleashed a vituperative campaign of character assassination. Bill Clinton was assailed by his detractors with stories of his marital infidelity and his twelve-year long affair with a cabaret artist Jennifer Flowers.[9] The New York tabloids *Star* and *Playboy* published interviews and excerpts of alleged taped conversations of Miss Flowers with Governor Clinton.[10] The opposition accused Mr. Clinton of his estrangement with his lawyer wife, Hillary Rodham. The smear campaign included an attack on Clinton's preference to the gay rights and abortion vitiating the cherished family values of the Americans.

The severe attack on his private life appeared to have caused a little setback to Mr. Clinton's ascendancy but did not menace his chances at the hustings.[11] In fact a cross section of the voters interviewed by independent pollster revealed that the majority of them were interested in "America beyond the bedroom." (*Newsweek*, 3 Feb. 1992, p. 19) Johno Sullivan, in his editorial in *National Review* (XLIV, 3, February 17, 1992), reflected the mood of the American electorate. He observed: "any sensible tax payer would much prefer to be governed by an adulteror of sound anti-inflationary views than by a socialist monk." As such, Bill

Clinton's chances could not be blunted by sex scandals.

However, the one issue that had "shaken" Clinton's candidacy and sought to sabotage his ambilition to get into the White House was "the Vietnam question."[12] The dramatic disclosure of Clinton's "evasion" of military service during the Vietnam war swung, albeit temporarily, the Democratic candidacy of Clinton into uncertainty. Mr. Clinton's letter to Col. Holmes thanking the latter "for saving" him from the draft and his purported intention of escaping from "the greatest chance of being drafted" by lying to the ROTC official in 1969 was leaked to the press "in a devastating piece of timing." It was intended to embarrass the Arkansas governor seeking support from the nation's first primary in New Hampshire.

The leak (February 6, 1992) and the subsequent denial of Mr. Clinton caused intense discussion in the country. The New-Hampshire voters rejected Mr. Clinton by preferring Paul Tsongas, former Senator from Massachusetts on Feburary 18, 1992 indicating their resentment to Mr. Clinton's character.[13] Ironically it was at the same place 24 years earlier (1968) the incumbent Democratic president Lynden B. Johnson suffered a severe beating for his "Americanization of the Vietnam war."[14]

The setback received by Mr. Clinton in New Hampshire engulfed his candidacy and the very elections in "Questions, questions, questions." The depth of the popular discontent over Clinton's "cloudy" role in the Vietnam draft may be gauged from an opinion poll taken by Gerry Chervinsky, a Boston poll taken for *The Boston Globe* and WBZ-TV.[15] Mr. Gerry Chervinsky observed: "The Vietnam question has allowed people who didn't want to admit they had problems with his personal life to move away from him – or at least take a second look."

As Daniel S. Papp had remarked: "a 'Vietnam' – even today, Americans often react to the work with mixed feelings of failure, frustration and guilt."[16] Therefore, it was natural to stir popular resentment with Bill Clinton with allegations of his "draft waffling." He was accused of "organizing demonstrations while in foreign land against your country [America] when young ghetto kids had been drafted and are dying."[17] Clinton was also charged with inconsistent statements on his draft status. President Bush alleged that Bill Clinton evaded straight answers to the questions whether Clinton obtained draft deferment or not, whether he secured induction notice or not, whether he intentionally misled the ROTC official or not, whether he met him personally or through some mediators or not. Bush lamented that Bill had often changed his statements and cryptically remarked: "that is the difference." It is this whiff of evasion agonized the voters. It was also pointed out that the American voters who (in 1992) preferred to "overlook his efforts to avoid service in an unpopular war" but they protested at Clinton's "inconsisent accounts about an important moment in his life."[18] Some voters were driven to the conclusion that "Clinton would say anything to get elect president."[19]

The trauma of Vietnam, as Bill Turque remarked, "is likely to be a minefield for candidates." However, Bill Clinton succeeded extricating himself from the setback he received in some of the primaries such as New Hampshire and Connecticut by the super Tuesday, March 10, 1992 when eleven states (mostly in the South) had voted in party polls.[20] Clinton's campaign managers meticulously planned the strategy to convert weakness, for strength. The alleged letter to Col. Holmes was fully released to the press and its moralistic content emphasized. The letter's strong points include Mr. Clinton's criticism of the draft and the war itself. He wrote: "I came to believe that the draft system itself is illegitimate. No government really rooted in limited, parliamentary democracy should have the power to make its citizens fight and kill and die in a war they may oppose." (*The New York Times*, 13 Feb. 1992, A 25) The most unpopular nature of the war was recognized when millions of Americans across the country wore black armbands on October 16, 1969 demanding an end to fighting in what was called Vietnam Moratorium. (*Ibid.*) Clinton was justified in his opposition to the Vietnam war because most of his contemporaries in college campuses[21] and in public life denounced the "unwanted war in Vietnam."[22] Prominent realists such as Hams Morgenthau, George Kennan, Reinhold Niebuhr and Walter Lippmann, among others, "condemned American participation in Vietnam."[23] It may not be out of place to mention that the opinion poll conducted in 1978 revealed that the Vietnam war was "more than a mistake, it was fundamentally wrong and immoral."

Robert McNamara, Secretary of State for Defence under Kennedy and Johnson (upto January 1968), justified Clinton's draft avoidance in his article of August 3, 1992. McNamara underscored the displeasure of majority of Americans like Bill Clinton over the legitimacy of the war. He observed: "But I write also to say that I knew then, and I know now, the anguish of those who honestly and sincerely—and perhaps correctly—opposed the war." He concluded his article with a significant statement: "We [should] respect those who agonized with grave doubts as to whether their nation was on a morally acceptable course."[24]

Mr· Clinton in his letter to Col. Holmes justified the draft and the American participation in World War II because "the life of the people collectively was at stake. Individuals had to fight, if the nation was to survive." (*The New York Times*, 13 Feb. 1992, A-17) Clinton repeated his assertion at a press conference in February 1992: "I supported the Persian Gulf war because I thought it was right and in our national interest, just as I opposed the Vietnam war because I thought it was wrong and not in our national interest. And I still think I was right." (*The New York Times*, 14 Feb. 1992, A-29) In his third television debate (October 1992) Clinton was able to turn the tide against his Vietnam bashers. He denied any credibility gap in his career and maintained that "going back 23 years ago, I don't know, I was opposed to the war. I could not help that. I felt very strongly about it."[25]

Bill Clinton's readiness to serve in Vietnam much against his conscience was reflected in his letter (September 12, 1969). He wrote: "After I signed the ROTC letter of intent I began to wonder whether the compromise I had made with myself was not more objectionable than the draft status and reinduction into active service. This decision, he pointed out, was prompted by his desire "to maintain my politics viability within the system. (*The New York Times*, 13 Feb. 1992, A-17) In other words "to prepare myself for a political life."

In spite of so much of furore over Clinton's Vietnamese connection, the American voters reposed their confidence in his leadership and his promise of halting the nation's slide in the economy. Clinton declared, "I just have to hope that people will judge me as a prospective commander-in-chief in the way they judge Dick Cheny (Secretary of Defence under President Bush) who had a (draft) deferment I just have to hope that [my past] will be seen in context." (*Newsweek*, 24 Feb. 1992, p. 22)

The American voters overwhelmingly responded to his plea for a change in the White House despite his Vietnamese nightmare. It only shows that the post-Vietnam war generation is less concerned with the failings of 60s than what happens today. As Nancy Bekavac pointed out: "Each generation has its war." (*The New York Times*, 31 March 1992, A-17) The election results showed that Bill Clinton secured most of the 20 percent new voters who exercised their franchise in November 1992, a majority of them are from minorities such as the African-Americans, the Laltinos and the hispanics. He also secured a significant proportion of inner city votes (45 percent) and majority of women's vote (51 percent). Interestingly Bill Clinton secured for the first time in 20 years industrial but of New England states including New Hampshire (where he lost in the Feburary primary). The Republican bastions in the pacific belt including California rallied to the support of Bill Clinton. His convincing margin of 100 electoral votes (370) over the required votes revealed the people's penchant for change notwithstanding the Vietnam imbroglio. It may be presumed that Americans may no longer be interested in the uses and abuses of the Vietnam war for settling domestic issues. Perhaps, Vietnam is fading into history as the post-cold-war president assumed office on January 20, 1993.

NOTES

1. *The Wall Street Journal*, February 6, 1992. The letter of December 3, 1969 sent from England was allegedly leaked by the Pentagon according to Clinton's manager David Wilhelm. However, Tedd Koppel of *Nightline* TV network revealed that the letter was disclosed by Col. Clinton Jones, a former Arkansas ROTC official. *The New York Times*, February 13, 1992, p. A 25, col. 1.
2. *Ibid.*
3. Carl N. Degler, *Out of Our Past*: *The Forces that Shaped Modern America* (Indian Rep., New Delhi, 1986), p. 549.
4. Clinton's letter to Col. Eugene Holmes, *The New York Times*, p. A 17, col. 3.
5. Saraswathi Krishna Kumar, "The Clinton Win—America's, Mandate for Change," *Frontline*, November 20, 1992, p. 9.
6. T.V. Parasuram, "People Politics," *The Week*, Jan. 17, 1993, p. 36.
7. C.T. Kurien, "Clinton and the U.S. Economy," *Frontline,* November 20, 1992, p. 132.
8. *Competition Success Review*, December 1992, p. 106.
9. J.O. Sullivan, "Don't say it with Flowers, *National Review*, February 24, 1992, p. 44.
10. Quoted in R. Behar, "Anatomy of Smear," *Time*, January 1992, pp. 34-35.
11. A. McCarthy, "The Character Issue," *Commonweal*, May 8, 1992, pp. 8-9.
12. Robin Toner, "Clinton's Candidacy is Shaken, Again," *The New York Times*, February 13, 1992, p. 25.
13. Stuart Gorin, *U.S. Elections' 92*, Feb. 19, 1992 (USIS Madras).
14. Arthur M. Schlesinger, ed., *History of American Presidential Elections 1789-1968*, vol. IV, p. 3717.
15. *The New York Times*, February 13, 1992, p. A 25.
16. *Vietnam*: *The View from Moscow, Peking, Washington* (Jefferson, 1981), p. 1.
17. P. George Bush, Televised Debate, October 19, 1992.
18. B. Turque, "Reliving the Sixties," *Newsweek*, Feb. 24, 1992, p. 17.
19. G.J. Church, "Questions, Questions," *Time*, April 20, 1992, pp. 41-42.
20. E. Drew "Letter from Washington," *The New Yorker*, April 20, 1992, p. 100.
21. Arthur M. Schelsinger, vol. IV, p. 3716. Allard K. Lowenstein, the

young New York lawyer and President, National Students Union, led massive student rallies against the Vietnam war in Democratic Los Angeles convention in July 1968.

22. *Ibid.*, Republican platform, p. 3793.
23. Arthur M. Schelsinger, *The Cycles of American History* (Boston, 1986), p. 76.
24. "On Avoiding Draft," *Newsweek*, August 3, 1992, p. 120.
25. Bill Clinton's Television Debate, October 19, 1992, Michigan, *USIS Wireless File*, October 19, 1992, p. 23.

American Presidential Elections, 1992

SUBHRAM RAJKHOWA

An election in any democratic country evinces keen interest among the citizens, who are called upon to decide the fate of political parties and government. This is more so in the case of a great democracy like the United States, for it evinces not only national interest but is keenly followed by the world community at large. This is because the United States is considered the world leader and its policies and programmes vitally affect both the international order as well as the nation states, and the leadership provided makes all the difference.

The United States Presidential election, 1992, for electing the 42nd President has been keenly followed the world over, more so, due to the changed world scenario ushering in a new world order and the varied issues involved. With regard to the domestic scene this election is being contested primarily on the vital issue of the American economy, engulfed as it is by a huge budget deficit of four trillion dollars. An added dimension has been the entry into the fray of an influential independent candidate who has been able not only to evoke the interest of the electors, but register his name in all the fifty states.

Coming to the electoral system, the most striking feature in the rules has been the adoption of the peculiar state-by-state sequence of direct primaries for the selection of Presidential candidates. The basic change is that Presidential nominations today are being made by primaries, albeit primaries that operate differently from those used by the States for other purposes. Parties hope to nominate candidates who are electable, representative of party views and able to govern. However, Presidential candidates run for office without exclusively relying on the party, by hiring media and campaign technicians and by making personal and issue-oriented appeals to voters. The people select a state of Presidential electors, equal to the number of Senators and Representatives each State has in the Congress. The candidate with the highest number of votes in each State wins all the electoral votes of the State. The electoral college is essentially a rubber stamp body that casts its electoral votes according to state results on winner take all basis.

The Presidential election campaign, extending for a major part of the year started with the primaries of the two main political parties, the Republican Party and the Democratic Party. For the Republicans, the nomination process was comparatively easy because of the announcement of candidature of President Bush, the present incumbent, who had an impressive record on the external front, with victory against Iraq and the cold war. Still, he had some anxious moments because of his performance on the domestic front. He was susceptible to protest vote which he had to weather in the primary due to the economic slowdown. But prior to the Republican primaries, it was the primaries of the Democratic Party that set the ball rolling for this election. The Democratic Presidential nominee Mr. Bill Clinton, the Governor of Arkansas, the longest serving Governor with a record of twelve years, announced his candidature on February 18, 1992. He entered his first primary in the New England State of New Hampshire along with five others, but manoeuvred his way to the Party nominatiion in spite of initial setback amidst reports of marital infidelity, doubts about his patriotism due to evasion of military duty during the Vietnam war and smoking of marijuana in his youth. His politics of compromise, determination and durability, organizing ability and money power saw him through the Party's nomination. He also had an impressive track record in the job and education front as the Governor in his State.

The nation saw the emergence of an influential independent candidate in Mr. Ross Perot, after long 64 years, who evoked considerable response from the voters. Among the 23 candidates in the fray, apart from Mr. Bush and Mr. Clinton, Mr. Perot's candidature evoked much interest, not for being the leading candidate, but for cutting into votes and tilting the balance. The Texas billionaire caused panic in both the Republican and Democratic camps with a serious bid for the White House and as an independent candidate was able to register his name in the ballot papers of all the fifty states. However, he threw in the towel before throwing the hat in the Presidential ring on July 16, 1992, only to re-enter at the penultimate stage contending, that both Mr. Bush and Mr. Clinton did not address the real issues. His main thrust was the budget deficit and that of providing employment, provoking a debate on debt reduction and the creation of jobs.

Separate political actors in two different groups gives the 'out' group the corporate identity to criticize the 'ins.' The 'ins' are thus forced to take responsibility, for and to defend their policies and programs, thus focussing public debate, thereby giving the electorate a chance to decide the course. Wtih the formal nomination of George Bush and Bill Clinton along with the entry of Ross Perot began the serious bid for the Presidency of the United States. The main issue bordering around the economy evoked much interest and provoked the candidates even to probe each other's honesty and leadership. This election also saw the increasing use of the electronic media starting with the free phone-in-and-phone-out calls campaign by Democratic party hopeful Jerry Brown to extensive television campaigns by Mr. Perot.

Mr. Clinton, the baby boomer, in his agenda held out promise of results over ideology or political party, stressing on economic growth, tax fairness, universal Health care, racial harmony and a lower federal budget deficit along wtih an assurance to rescind President Bush's ban on abortions at federally funded clinics, allow unpaid family emergency leave, regulate cable TV, and to admit homosexuals to the military. While criticizing the Republicans for refusing to harness the power of Governemnt to cure the nation's domestic ills, he advocated personal responsibility and smaller federal bureaucracy. On the foreign policy front he expressed his desire to support the West Asia peace initiative of President Bush, extend aid to Russia, avoid US troops' involvement in Yugoslavia, cut size of American troops in Europe, set up United Nations' rapid deployment of force, cut defence spending by 100 billion dollars and link human rights abroad to trade concessions.

President Bush, the triumphant leader of the Gulf war with a popularity rating of over ninety percent after the war, claimed credit for US leadership over the Western alliance, end of the cold war, West Asia peace initiatives and focussed his experience at the Oval office, but had no credible answer to the nation's economic ills which was reeling under a four trillion dollar debt. He attributed the economic scene as part of a world-wide recession. He did not attempt to spark the faltering economy in 1991 with tax cuts and job spending. He was slow and reluctant to respond to the recession. This perhaps attributed to his not so impressive campaign in spring. Mr. Bush gained in the ratings when he stopped being defensive and launched a frontal attack on Mr. Clinton, hammering. the favourite theme of trust and accusing the Democrat as a deft dodger, evasive, lax and spend no gooder. He dubbed Mr. Perot as paranoid and frightening, while the latter accused him of playing dirty tricks, even going to the extent of threatening to affect his daughter's marriage prospects. Perot's main theme was the economy and he advocated increase in taxes, decrease in Government spending on programmes that are costly. His thrust on the deficit and that of providing employment provoked a debate on debt reduction and the creation of jobs.

With the withdrawal of Mr. Perot from the contest in mid-July, mutual attacks between Mr. Bush and Mr. Clinton gained in vigour with the former lashing out at the record of his opponent for promising the moon when on issue after issue the sky had fallen in his own backyard and of delivering misery at home! He said, 'Once you buy what he is selling, there is no refund.' The latter mocked at the President for ducking a public debate with him under the pretext that he is not acceptable. Mr. Bush claimed that his was the only agenda that includes cutting the size of the Government and reducing the Federal deficit in order to provide for a prosperous America, criticizing Mr. Clinton for offering more of old big taxes, big Government with no serious plan to control the deficit. Mr. Clinton alleged Mr. Bush of playing in election year farm politics by waiting until before the elections to expand export incentives to wheat farmers, terming talk about expanded trade as an instance of opportunistic policy, criticizing him for failure to prod European countries to accept American pork and other farm products. Both of them tried to win over Mr. Perot's supporters by selling his fifty coordinators on their respective economic plans, and by attempting to smooth feelings ruffled after Mr. Perot abandoned his bid in July.

However, Mr. Perot re-entered the contest, further confounding the scene by claiming that he had answer to the economic issues and that both the Republican and Democrat did not properly address the 350 million dollar Federal deficit. He said before his re-entry that he did not want the job and suggested that he was more interested in qualifying for equal TV time and favourable rates to air issue-oriented campaign advertisements.

The last few weeks saw the election campaign at its peak with the three rounds of TV debates, hectic tours of States, even by buses and train to establish closer contacts with the electorate. There was a sea-change in techinque – newspapers, news magazines and TV network news shows were used. The role of the mediators, the analyst, the political commentator had been diminished.

The debate by Mr. Larry King on 'Media vs. Bias' and that of Mr. David Frost were marked by contrasting styles, with the former warming the three candidates and drawing Bush into doing dirt on Clinton, Vietnam, in a way damaging to himself. Frost could bring a tragic divinity to Clinton's loss on Vietnam experience – a loss of rite of passage – memory at the same time chastizing Perot for his 'irresponsibility' in making sleazy accusations which lacked objectivity.

The question of media bias was started by 'Star' involving Jennifer Flowers, night club singer, as Clinton's lover, followed by CNN journalists alleging Bush's affair with a diplomat. The news of Bush's Iraq gate and Iran gate affairs led to decline in his poll ratings. All these provoked the candidates to remark the election as 'unpleasant and ugly.'

Mr. Bush, on the trail in opinion polls, claimed in September that he had the right proposals and being on the right track for holding the line and reducing taxes would finally succeed, since Mr. Clinton did not have the right policies.

The three Presidential debates turned lively and its impact was very much evident in the initial one, followed by Mr. Clinton and President Bush. According to opinion polls, Mr. Clinton emerged the winner in the second debate. The debate in Richmond was a spirited one. Provoked by questions from the audience and being reminded of their concerns and disinterest in mutual mud slingings, the debate focussed on the main issues. Mr. Bush, trailing in opinion polls, failed to lend the crushing blows needed to resuscitate the campaign. While he accused Mr. Clinton of organizing anti-Vietnam war demonstrations, Mr. Clinton termed him a political chameleon. With all three claiming solutions to the country's economic ills, the viewers keenly watched their moves. Mr. Bush claimed that given a chance he will fix the economy by decreasing taxes and lessening government regulation. Mr. Clinton promised creation of jobs, improvement in education and to balance the budget in contrast to the 'trickle down economies' practised by Reagan-Bush administration. Mr. Perot criticized the hold of special interest groups on the legislators and promised to devote him every minute in creating jobs and rekindling the hope that succeeding generation would fare better than the first. According to opinion polls Mr. Clinton was expected to take most of the large States having large number of votes. But Mr. Bush vowed to prove the poll stars wrong by pulling off the political upset of the century. In the last of the presidential debates, organized by an independent commission, although Mr. Bush was more positive, the day belonged to Mr. Clinton.

In the final week, Mr. Bush managed to garner increasing support but for revelation of the United States' role in Iraq suffered a setback. Mr. Clinton had a three point lead over Mr. Bush down from the double digit margin several weeks ago. Mr. Bush harked back to President Truman's whistle stop tours as he travelled by train hammering the favourite theme of trust and experience, but in the end the day belonged to Mr. Clinton.

The tide of economic discontent in the United States Presidential campaign found reflection on third November, when Mr. Clinton secured 365 of the 538 electoral votes. He emerged victorious in eleven North East States, most of the West and the industrial States of Illinois, Michigan and Ohio. A change in the traditional key strongholds proved a gain for the Democrats. Mr. Clinton secured 43% compared to 38% for Bush and 19% for Mr. Perot, the highest by an independent in sixty four years.

The thirty two year decline in voter turnout was reversed by the participation of one hundred million voters. The economic depression might have been responsible for the increase in voter registration in nine of the ten jurisdictions which might have been the result of discontent among voters, thus accounting for the higher turnout.

The electorate responded to Mr. Clinton's claim as candidate of change and a new generation, who vowed to create more jobs, reduce the federal deficit and help restore the stalled economy. His vow to solve problems too long ignored from the economy to AIDS and environment appealed to the voters in spite of his being rated behind both Mr. Bush and Mr. Perot on the honesty and integrity front. Perot lost but excited some people who might otherwise have turned off the two parties.

The election will go down in history as a media election par excellence as the electronic media has brought electrol politics alive as never before. At the same time the campaign was a brutal one marked by charges by each candidate that his opponent could not be trusted. It has proved that a triumphant leader of war need not necessarily be the best leader to deal with problems of peace.

The Basic Dilemma of American Foreign Policy

HARENDRA MEHTA

American foreign policy like the foreign policy of any sovereign nation is the product of its national orientation. When we spell out the objectives of the American nation as recorded in the Preamble to the US constitution, we gather what is the orientation of the American nation. It is this orientation which, in the final analysis, should propel American foreign policy.

To say that the foreign policy of a nation subserves its national interest is misleading oversimplification. While the national interest is a powerful determinant of the foreign policy, it is not the sole determinant. A nation, like a human person, has a personality. It has its material needs no doubt; but it has its spiritual cravings, its requirement of self-fulfilment.

Supposedly, the American nation has an isolationist orientation. A revealing sample of the thinking of the American people on the matters of foreign policy is found in the following quotation in the book of Temple Wanamaker: "The Secretary of State received this telegram from a man in South Carolina. Very much opposed to your meddling in foreign affairs. Why don't we mind our own business?" This rhetorically asked question is answered by Wanamaker himself. He observes that the sentiment of the concerned citizen "would strike a responsive chord in many a citizen." He answers the question by a lucid elucidation. Foreign affairs has been defined as the activities of a nation, arising from its dealings with other nations. A nation can't help being involved in foreign affairs unless it is able to seal itself off from the rest of world, as did Japan, before 1853. Having come to the conclusion that foreign affairs and impliedly foreign policy are the necessary business of the United States, he further observes, "I believe we would agree with the drafters of the Constitution that among our proper concerns are 'to form a more perfect Union, establish Justice, insure domestic tranquillity, provide for the common defence, promote the General Welfare and secure the Blessings of Liberty to ourselves and our Posperity." Meeting these concerns would seem to be our business. The world is now so inter-related that events anywhere can have an effect upon our domesic tranquillity, defence, welfare and liberty. Minding our business, therefore, means being very much concerned with what is happening abroad and, where advisable and possible taking action."[1] It is the last part of the observation that should interest and concern us, that is too say, the instances when the United States concerned itself with what happened abroad in the years following the end of the cold war and thereabout and when it thought it desirable and possible to take action. With all its unrivalled military might daunting strike-power of its forces, the United States has its limitations just as the most formidable-looking knight has the chink in his armour.

While it is true that the isolationist streak in the minds of the American people remains ever present thought in a dormant form, II World War and its aftermath made isolationism rather irrelevant to the formulation and execution of American foreign policy. The period immediately following II World War established the United States as militarily most powerful nation in the world with the monopoly of the most devastating nuclear arsenal and an economy practically free from ravages of war. It is a significant fact of enormous importance that the United States is the only combatant-nation of II World War which did not witness the war on its own soil. That is perhaps an additional factor which nursed the illusion in the American people that they are indeed the God's chosen people. This is in no small measure a factor which has prompted the United States to dictate its norms, way of life and conditions on the people of other races sometimes in utter disregard of the fact that such way of life norms and conditions were detrimental to the interests of those races and, much worse, such norms, conditions and way of life were considered derogatory to their own personalities by those ethnic nations. The basic principles of American foreign policy were formulated on the basis of the 'superior nation' syndrome which has of course a substantial parentage. We may note the observations of a member of the Protestant clergy made a century earlier. Josiah Strong wrote: "Every race which has deeply impressed itself on human family has been the representative of some great idea – one or more – which has given direction to the nation's life and from it to civilization . . . but it was left for the Anglo-Saxon branch fully to recognize the right of the individual to himself and formally to declare it the foundation-stone of the government . . . but, I believe, it is fully in the hands of Christians of the United States next fifteen or twenty years to hasten or retard the coming of Christ's kingdom in the world by hundreds, and perhaps by thousand years. We of this generation and nation occupy the Gibraltar of the ages which commands the world's future."[2] The outstanding fact is that the Reverend has mentioned the significant ideas of Egyptians, of Presians, of Hebrews but not of Hindus or the Chinese, the two intensely ancient civilizations. This is constant failing of the Americans which has marred seriously the formulation and execution of foreign policy founded on the perceptions developed during the post-war years. Charleas Bohlen very rightly observes: "The Second World War made a tremendous impact on American foreign policy, and it followed that the years 1947-48, the years of decision provided the basis of what now is our foreign policy and the world role. But first of all, consider the historic tradition. The United States for over 150 years had lived under the admonition contained in George Washington's Farewell address in September 1796 in which he warned the people of the United States to beware of involvement in European affairs."[3]

However history testifies that the admonition was found impracticable and never totally honoured. But the spectacular transformation of the United States into an industrial giant by the end of the nineteenth century made the admonition almost irrelevant. One may also observe that the transformation was accomplished on the basis of the tremendous agricultural surplus created by the Negro slaves and the vast farms brought under the control of the white farmers by the systematic decimation of the Red Indian race. The participation in I World War, brief reversal to Isolationism followed by the gradual entry into the world politics under FDR and involvement in II World War and assumption of the prime actor's role during the cold war years gave the world an opportunity to view the American nation's orientation. Through many turns and twists stretching over four decades and more of the cold war, the world and particularly the Third World could not discern the traces of the idealism of the Preamble to the Constitution. The basic dilemma of American foreign policy is that the sterling commitment to humanism expressed in the preamble appears totally stifled in its projection in the relations between the nations. The factors that can be held responsible for this dilemma are identifiable.

Firstly, the overwhelming White component of the American nation has disabled the formulators and executors of American foreign policy from appreciating the values and traditions of the other races. The observations of the Protestant priest Josiah Strong quoted earlier represent the eternal view of the American people about other people and about their 'divine' mission to impose their view on society, politics and economy the world over. In the so-called unipolar world after the end of cold war resulting from the collapse of the USSR, this imposition is pushed with greater vigour and determination. The US insistence on the adoption of the patents laws of its choosing on India is a case in point. The great oration of Swami Vivekananda a hundred years ago should have made Americans aware of the breadth and vision of Indian culture. All

Americans are not cast in the mould of Josiah Strong, the Protestant priest. The liberal minds of the United States are very much aware of the immense contribution of the Indian culture to the human civilization. Will Durant, the preeminent sociologist observes: "Nothing should more deeply shame the modern student than the inadequacy of his acquaintance with India. . . . An impressive continuity of development and civilization from Mohenjo Daro 2900 BC or earlier to Gandhi, Raman and Tagore; faiths compassing every stage from barbarous idolatory to most subtle and spiritual pantheism; philosophers playing a thousand variations on the monistic theme from the Upanishads eight centuries before Christ to Shankara eight centuries after him; scientists developing astronomy three thousand years ago, and winning prizes in our time; a democratic constitution of untraceable antiquity in the villages and wise and beneficent rulers like Ashoka and Akbar in the capitals; minstrels singing great epics almost as old as Homer and poets holding world audiences today. . . . This is the India that patient scholarship is now opening up, like a new intellectual continent, to the Western mind which only yesterday thought civilization an exclusively European thing."[4]

To this one may add that the Indian epics like the *Ramayana* and the *Mahabharata* differ from Homer's *Iliad* in an important manner. They continue to provide the ethical guidelines to the poor and illiterate to this day and have helped Hinduism to dispense with the established Church and the Sunday schools and preserve its proverbial immortality.

When the American foreign policy makers formulate their strategy in regard to such a nation, they should not lose sight of the fact that a particular policy offered to India should be in accordance with its cultural enviornment. No eco-legal measure is culturally natural – a measure like patent (in regard to so-called TRIPS). The post-cold war period has witnessed increasing pressure on India, for example, in this area under the guise of the Dunkel draft proposals. A *Times of India* columnist sympathetic to the new market-friendly policies of the present government in India writes: "Another area where the draft is unfavourable to India is trade-related intellectual property rights (TRIPS). If the draft is accepted, India will have to change its patent laws. It will have to allow product patents instead of process patents and the period for the product-patents will have to be increased to 20 years from the seven years allowed at present. This will prevent Indian companies from developing alternative chemical processes to make drugs patented by multinationals. As a result prices of new drugs developed by multinationals will rise although it will affect only a small sector at the upper end of the market."[5] The rise in prices estimated by the writer is, for obvious reasons on the low side. The rise in prices is likely to be of the order of at least four hundred percent with a staggering effect on the life-expectancy of the poor. The multinationals are already flushed with profits. But that may not concern the mandarins of the State Dept. But equally significant is the fact, if not more, that in India intellectuals of the ancient times Aryabhatts, Varahmihir or Shankara did not claim any property rights on their intellectual attainment nor some of the most miraculous remedies of Ayurveda which amazed the American medical opinion were ever patented. The basic ideas in mathematics and even religion were nurtured in India and transmitted to the West through the medium of the Arabs. These ideas form the bedrock of Western science and technology of which the United States is a great beneficiary. The United States owes an incalculable debt to India. But such moral considerations are alien to the hard bargainers like Carla Hill. But a question can be posed. How far this thorough-going 'economism' can sustain the mutual give-and-take which the new-fangled globalism undoubtedly dictates?

Secondly one cannot sidetrack from one's mind as citizen of State belonging to exploited and deprived South the immeasurable distances in standard and style of life that divide India from the United States. These distances can be penpictured in the most hurting way. Economically, India does not bear any comparison to America or other rich countries either in terms of National Income or Gross National Product. "With less than 6% of the world's population, Americans consume about 60% of the goods and developed resources of the world. . . . In the Vietnam War—the war which was never declared a national war by the Congress . . .—$ 25 billion a year were spent for many years. This amount is about $2\frac{1}{2}$ times the total budget of India. In fact America spends more on advertising, or cosmetics, or smoking than India . . . spends in a year on all national projects. . . . Americans spend less of their disposable income on food (16.8) than any other nationality."[6] But this residence on the summit of economic prosperity does not afford happiness to the United States as the Marlen Brando starrer 'The Last Tango in Paris' displaying the surfeit of food and sex in the Eastern world projected. The social life of the United States is one of the most miserable by the usual cultural norms based on the state of institutions of marriage and family. "The American families are in trouble—trouble so deep and pervasive as to threaten the future of our nation (White House Conference on Children). . . . But in view of the high and increasing rate of divorce, separation, desertion and the families headed by women who never married, the notion of American family as mummy, a daddy and 2, 4 two heads . . . today looks particularly fictitious (*Time*, December 24, 1973). . . . We are witnessing a population explosion of 'Solos' people who live alone."[7]

Let us digest the fact that American foreign policy through the agreement that it forces on the third world is trying to sell the so-called American way of life in disregard of the necessities and compulsions of the economies of the third world. The terms and conditionalities of the IMF such as the reduction in the coverage of the public distribution services by India, the removal of import-control are the measures which are politically infeasible and their efficacy untested and well in doubt. They may even cripple the economy of India. According to Medha Patkar, the enviromentalist, under the Dunkel programme the Indian agriculturist would be just the handy-man of the multinational. Most particularly, these proposals recommend a programme which would certainly frustrate the objectives of justice and welfare enshrined in the Preamble to the Constitution supposed to be the bedrock of American foreign and domestic policies.

Thirdly, the legitimacy of violence that has engulfed the minds of the American nation is transmitted into their foreign policy. All major crises of the American nation have been solved through widespread use of violence. The War of Independence was fought on the issue which could have been solved through statesmanlike pressures on the British Crown and the parliament. It started the American people on their career as a nation. The maintenance of slavery entailed continuous violence or the threat of its use. The issue of racial equality was resolved through a longdrawn, internecine war. Let us not sidetrack the fact that it is this war which finally stabilized 'the indestructible union of the indestructible states.' Eighty years later the use of the nuclear device to defeat half-vanquished enemy in defiance of the norms of international law; that law requires the combatants to warn the adversary of the devastation of a new weapon which, of course, President did not think of doing. There was also a racial arrogance in this action. The British Military writer B.H. Liddell later charged that the United States would never have used the bomb against the white people in Berlin.[8] The horrors sanctioned as the wherewithal of American foreign policy in Vietnam are too well-known and agonizing to be described in detail. The use of most modern weapons and display of air power to save the Republican Administration from the unpopularity of the 'body-bags' count in the gulf war immediately after the liquidation of the cold war too has its basis of racial consideration.

With this 'unenviable' record, to put it rather mildly, American foreign policy cannot even be expected to come near the noble sentiments expressed in Preamble to Constitution. I believe the spirits of Thomas Paine, of Thomas Jefferson, of Woodrow Wilson and FDR wherever they are resting would not be resting in peace; that of Lincoln would have shifted by now his resting place to Afro-Asian soil.

These three considerations outlined here – the disability of the

American nation to comprehend the cultures of the other races particularly of those with roots in hoary past like that of India, its inability to understand the economic disabilities of the nations of the third world—the victims of the most dehumanized system of control of one nation by another called Imperialism, and finally the overwhelming and widening legitimacy of violence in the domestic and foreign policy has created an incorrigible dilemma for American foreign policy. It cannot achieve the objectives contained in Preamble to the US Constitution.

This phenomena holds an important guideline for India which has embarked on the so-called market friendly policies, partially if not wholly under the IMF imprimatur.

(i) It has to consider the Dunkel proposals pushed forward by the West with extreme care as the West led by the USA have a scant understanding of the mores of the Indian society and the demands of its polity.

(ii) The unequal NPT should never be signed in its present form. India in probable cooperation with China should seek its drastic revision when it comes for revision in a couple of years.

(iii) The 'unipolar' world with US hegemony is unnatural: it is also detrimental to the sustenance of the peaceful and cooperative world order. India in close concert with Russia, China and third world countries of friendly orientation should modify it. Of course it would be a slow and tortuous process which has to be continuously propelled.

NOTES

1. *American Policy Today* (New York: Bantam, 1964), p. 3.
2. *Our Country: Its Possible Future and Present Crisis* (New York: Baker and Taylor, 1885), pp. 159 and 180.
3. *Transformation of Ameican Foreign Policy* (New York: W.W. Norton, 1969), p. 11
4. *Our Oriental Heritage* (New York: Simon and Shuster, 1954), p. 391.
5. Vivek Bharati, "Dunkel in Perspective: Rejection is not an Option," *Times of India*, 3 Feb. 1992.
6. Surinder Gupta, *Glimpses of Western World* (New Delhi: Amrit, 1985), pp. 9-10
7. *Ibid.*, p. v.
8. Stephen E. Ambrose, *Rise to Globalism—American Foreign Policy Since 1938* (New York: Penguin, 1983), p. 89.

End of the Cold War and American Foreign Policy

V.P. GAUR

An atmosphere of cold war had been gradually developing since the end of II World War. Says Palmer, "The strange allies of that war became the leaders of a bipolar world, locked in protracted conflict which assumed the form of a cold war."[1] Since then with the passage of time the cold war became 'colder.' The nature of the cold war has been given different interpretations by various writers. Some feel that it gives expression to two incompatible ways of life, democracy and communism. Others like Arnold Toynbee give a bi-polar interpretation to the conflicts of the cold war days. Toynbee is of the opinion that there were only two powers that mattered in the world, the USA and the USSR. It was indeed a fact of international politics that most of the states in the world were on the side of either Washington or Moscow. Of course, the really non-aligned states were to be excluded from this list. The non-aligned states and a few others like France wished to follow a completely independent policy. Of course, it would be difficult to retain that stance in the event of an international conflict.

In those days of tension and mutual internal hatred the scope of non-alignment was severely limited. As a matter of fact India had begun to follow the policy of non-alignment because of economic and political problems. In the seventies India's non-alignment appeared to have been dilated when it had come closer to the USSR and moved away from the USA. The western camp began to seriously doubt India's policy of non-alignment.

Despite the necessity of a firm stand in favour of one or the other, there has been a rift within both the American and the Russian camps. A few countries did not want to participate in the general orchestra, the tune of which was set by Washington or Moscow. They come forward with their original tunes which were jarring for the Super-Powers. Marshal Tito revolted with success against the political hegemony of the Soviet Russia, while France differed from the policies of the USA but it did not mean a major internal breach. In the Communist camp the revolts of Poland and Hungary were curbed successfully and upheavals in Czechoslovakia could not be capitalized by the western world. France under De Gaulle had begun to dream of an independent Europe. Though serious cracks had begun to appear in the Western camp, they were repaired on time when Nixon took a stiff stand on the US policy towards Western Europe. The NATO was saved and the temporary rift did not split up to an irreparable extent.

'The internal rift in the Communist camp between the Peoples' Republic of China and Soviet Russia was a major development in this field which provided a new dimension to the continuing cold war. It was a super conflict between two states, the USSR and the Communist China, projecting the same political ideology. Within the Communist camp two separate lines of action developed and their centres were Moscow and Peking.

Very strange sort of partnership began to develop in politics. The Communist Russia was finding more in common with democratic India while the Communist China was coming closer to its erstwhile enemy, the democratic USA. It also began to develop good relations with Pakistan. Thus the atmosphere of the cold war created a vicious climate in world politics.

The cold war came to an end with the fall of Soviet Russia as a Super Power. Historically international politics is based on the national self-interest and an alliance system and balance of power which create stability in world affairs. A balance on the global plane can be maintained by strengthening the UN efforts vis-a-vis the unilateral approach of the US in areas of conflict as in the Gulf crisis and various problems in Africa etc. Globalism has become imperative if humanity has to survive and live in peace. The piling of nuclear weapons by different powers also poses a very great challenge to the existing civilization. The US has to give up its previous stance of using force to settle different problems in favour of non-violent resolution of the conflicts. The UN had come into existence to establish peace but its efforts were crippled by the intense rivalry of the two Super Powers of the cold war. This atmosphere effected the deliberations in the UN forums also. So the globalism advanced by the UN will need supporters who are committed to a peaceful approach and non-violent politics and who will refrain from exploiting the UN forums also. So the globalism advanced by the UN will need supporters who are committed to a peaceful approach and non- violent politics and who will refrain from exploiting the UN for narrow national interests.

The end of the cold war removed the primary rationale that had brought about the Non-Aligned movement. Now the world scenario has changed. The Non-Aligned movement was anti-imperialist in its approach. It is less viable in the 1990s than it was during the 1960s and 1970s. The Non-Aligned Movement has survived without a viable justification and is thus ripe for revision or extinction. If it is wound up, the responsibility of the US will be more challenging in the post-cold war era. Europe may emerge in a new form and other centres of power might be established in the world.

When the cold war finally ended after continuing in a fierce form for about forty-five years, the natural consequence was defeat of one side and victory of the other. Victory could be defined as a mutual adjustment and accommodation between the contending parties. A sort of recognition of some sphere of influence of Russia in the Central Europe and America's close relations with western European countries have to be emphasized, in this respect.

The task of American foreign policy will really be challenging. The disintegration of the Soviet Union should bring about the end of the hegemonistic trends of the old Russian empire. The collapse of communism should help America in bringing about a gradual transition to democracy and a Free World.

The US foreign policy experts have to establish their greater credibility by supporting the UN actions. They have not to go ahead unilaterally in tackling different problems in the world by bypassing the UN. They have to proceed further under the umbrella of the UN whether it is the Gulf war or crisis in Lebanon or a problem in Asia or Africa. The UN organization and its agencies have to be strengthened in order to function effectively and efficiently in the pursuit of world peace. All problems should be taken to the UN forums and settled and solved there. There should be effective use of the International Court of Justice and different States must learn to respect its decisions. Humanity today is faced with many socio-cultural, economic and political problems. All of them can be effectively solved with confidence if the UN and its agencies are respected and strengthened. The financial institutions like the World Bank and the IMF should also be encouraged and helped.

America must find a good circle of friends which can together solve and settle problems peacefully. The atmosphere of distrust and hatred should yield place to that of goodwill and friendship. Weapons of destruction which were produced during the cold war have to be eliminated. Politics of cooperation instead of confrontation has to be followed. There is an imperative necessity of cautious vigilance. Even then prospects of a precarious peace are heightened by the possibility of irreparable danger to mankind by a future war because there would be no victory in such a war. World wars are unleashed only when policy makers on either side are persuaded that victory is possible. Man should try to rise above the feelings of jealousy, hatred and fear and by so doing, he should try to save his culture from being destroyed by the virus of animosity. If it is done, humanity will march towards peace and prosperity.

NOTE

1. Norman D. Palmer, Howard C. Perkins, *International Relations* (Calcutta, 1970), p. 758.

US Foreign Policy after the Cold War

GITANJALI DASH

American foreign policy is based on realism and imperialism and in post-World War II era the principal objective of it was the containment of communism. The American objective was to spread the message of democracy and free enterprise in contradiction to the Russian concept of egalitarian socialism.

Critics of the United States globalism often recall George Washington's "farewell address" which worked future American governments not to become involved in power, politics and the entangling alliance of the European statecraft and preached a modest republican isolationism.[1] But George Washington's idea of the pioneer in basic foreign policy-making of America was also the man who called the United States a "new empire" and dreamed of incorporating the entire new world into it and acting as a symbol for all government raised after the devastation of Europe's atavistic monarchies. Washington's warning against entangling alliances have more to do with his vision of American uniqueness and fate than they have to do with any modesty. The United States was a new type of nation, a moral nation, that should not sully itself in Europe's deceitful bickering.

After World War II, the US started massive aid programme under Marshal plan and Truman doctrine under the condition that only the nations who had joined the military alliances viz. NATO, GENTO, SEATO would get the aid. Thus America exported military sentiments under the guise of aid. Of course, popular opinion about commission need not matter very much as long as American foreign policy had other legitimations. Many realists argue that American foreign policy-maker would have to be anti-Soviet because the Soviet Union was the only major challenge to the United States left after the war and the US had not enough reason to be anti-Soviet. President Truman's personal speeches and writings, for instance, did not become strongly anti-Soviet and anti-Communist until he developed the conviction that the United States would have to replace British power throughout a major part of the world.[2]

Yet distrust and hatred for Communism has always been more than just a tactical necessary of Realpolitic, for many American decision-makers. For those with strong religious convictions, it fit on the top of and helped define the moral mission, that United States was expected to carry out. For instance, J. Edgar Hoover, the leader of the FBI for most of its existence and the one bureaucrat to whom everybody feared, was of deep conviction that the United States was special instrument chosen by God to contain world-communism.[3]

With the anti-communism already in place as a religious value of some American leaders, it has always been tempting for American national security managers to play upon popular religious and quasi-religious sentiments to sell, what otherwise might be unpopular imperial policies as part of an anti-communist crusade. Without the communists menace as a whole, a host of American post-war policies from the Marshall plan to military assistance given to repressive regimes throughout the Third World might never have surmounted the hurdles of public opinion even though those hurdles are very low.[4]

Even with all these innovations in American foreign policy, the new importance of the faith in science, realism and anti-communism, it is pertinent to emphasize how much did not change when the United States finally became a great power. Most significantly, American foreign policy-makers continued to define the core of national interest as an interest in "open doors" equal or better access for Americans to foreign markets[5] and sources of supply and to formulate the American dream that they were extending to the world in terms of the entire range of nineteenth-century liberal-economic principles including the defence of private property and special usefulness of markets.

The crisis in American supremacy in the 1970s threatened an American dream. The bloc that became the basis for American hegemony extended overseas, gaining the allegiance of government officials and eventually much of the bourgeoisie of Europe and Japan through the American post-war assistance policies and the successful establishment of a climate in which highly profitable capital economic growth could be expected.[6]

This development too had its ideological as well as material side. Intergovernmental institutions encouraging and monitoring government to government co-operation among developed market states – including the OECD, the Bank for International settlements, the GATT and the Bretton Woods Institutions – helped develop shared economic expectations among the United States and its allies. These institutions can be thought of as a special part of international 'civil society' even though they have some 'governmental' power, especially in relation to their third world members.

The neo-realists admit that certain short-term, reversible factors contributed to the US decline – the American public reluctance to use force in the third world after Vietnam war and the increase in Soviet military capabilities in the 1970s – but nothing can change the overall trend.[7]

One of the lessons of Vietnam to Henry Kissinger was that such deep involvement in the third world conflicts was counter-productive, a view that fit with Kissinger's desire to de-emphasize the third world. Many commentators, especially in the third world argued that this new policy was simply a consequence of the American-Soviet detente. If the Superpowers could co-operate they no longer needed to test each other's power in the third world. But Nixon's desire to ignore the third world was as much a cause of its interest in detente as it was a consequence. Beyond that, Kissinger's realism told him that the US needed very few friends in the third world. Third world states were just not powerful enough to affect American interests except when they were aided by other great power, as had been the case in Vietnam.[8] Kissinger of course had a bit more interest in the third world in his career.[9]

America's inability to protect allies from oil shocks shook American power in the Europe as well. However, it united with Europe to counter OPEC's barriers and restrictive policies. Oil crisis 1973 and 1979 were major blows to the hegemony of the US.

The immediate reason why the US unlike other democratic market countries,[10] failed to respond more positively to the NIEO was simply ideological. The simplistic economic liberalism that has always been an important guide to US foreign policy could not accept the global Keynesianism underlying the third world's demands, American policy makers could not accept the idea that governments needed to intervene in the world economy became large in investors, left together, fail to make the most profitable international investments possible and then systematically under- privileged the non-industrialized world.

The dramatic events that occurred in the Soviet Union in August 1991 shook not only the Soviet Union but sent its electrifying resounding waves in the whole world. One of the two superpowers was shattered badiy, receding the much-used term 'cold-war' into oblivion and Reagan's charge of Communist Russia as "evil empire" came to an end. Gorbachev's 'Perestroika' and 'Glasnost' had made him popular worldwide even though he was removed from power in his own country. The Soviet Union and its constituent states signed a new union treaty. Five out of fifteen republics remained out of the new arrangements.

The weakening of the Soviet Union has again made the US the undisputed and only Superpower to shape the world as per its wishes.[11] But the main fulcrum of new world order stability which the US was championing received a setback especially after the gulf war.

It is true that December 1991 war between the US and its allies against Saddam Hussein's attack over Kuwait has added some prestige to George Bush and America dictated over Iraq in stern terms charging Iraq against violation of 'Human Rights.' At the same time, America though somewhat relieved of Russia's eclipse as a world force, grew apprehensive of the pan-Islamic unity and integration of the Muslim community. Now the US is not so closed to Pakistan as it was in earlier days. Rather it tries to build up the ties with China, which started in 1971. Now China is coming up as a super power.

Will there be another Arab-Israeli war? The possibility cannot be ruled out as Saddam Hussein started winking once again. Throughout the 1980s the USA and the USSR continue to rival each other for influence in the third world. While the USSR has maintained military support for the third world, the USA invaded Granada, bombing Libya, arming anti-Soviet rebels in Cambodia, Afghanistan, Nicaragua and denying peace for Arab-Palestinians.

Recent events particularly the Zionist-US threat against the Arab and deliberate influence of Soviet Jews into occupied Arab- Palestinian territories in Israel rightly represent the state of Super-power gamble in West Asian world. It is no more Zionist-US axis against the Arabs but Zionist-US-Soviet axis that dictates terms to Arab-Palestinian.[12]

Now the Soviet Union has given rise to a new era of inequilibrium both politically and militarily. The US is worried about the formation of a giant Islamic belt. Now the US has bent down to aid Soviet Union economically, even the US allies in Western Europe also prefer this. Russia has joined the World Bank and the IMF Russia is being treated as developing country status. This shows American leniency towards economic reform in Russia. Even though, Yeltsin's economic reform is not upto the mark and the USA is not very happy about it. Even Russians are not happy with Yelstin's policies. So any change in Russia cannot be ruled out. The situation is very fluid and nothing can be predicted.

Divided Germany was a cause of tension in Europe. Kohl-Mitterand declaration of April 90 aimed at creation of the political union including common security institutions. The EEC started as economic community service, economic interest of Europe. Reunification of Germany accelerated and expedited the growth as a political union. But how responsible United Germany will be in a global context in a politically integrated Europe? In Persian Gulf crisis American-German differences surface threatening the coalition arrangement. But the question arises will the US and the unified Germany behave in consonance with the US wishes always converging a common ground to offer collective security to Europe or would it be an alternative structure to NATO? Does the growth of Franco-German brigade symbolize emergency in powers in Paris and Berlin as an independent power bloc?[13] The answer to these remain unanswered as Europe's situation remains fluid. The case of EEC over Maastricht Treaty proved this. Japan does not claim the same status as does Germany in Europe.

Japan's emergence as a financial super-power has many advantages to LDCs because of increasing technical and monetary assistance, grants-in-aid. Japan's ODA increase in 1986-92 was $ 50 million which was the largest in the world surpassing the US budgets.[14] Now-a-days Japan is coming up as a great nuclear power and ready to help the third world with isotopes and heavy water and other infrastructure. Some critics argue Japan maintains a distance from the third world and is more close to USA to expand its markets and trading activities. But the recent grants-in-aid of Japan to LDCs disprove this. In February 1989, India got grants-in-aid worth 1109 million yen. Recently also the Prime Minister P.V. Narasimha Rao visited Japan and was successful in getting Japanese collaboration. Japan is also giving massive aid to sub-Saharan Africa.

The greatest peril is not from the United Germany nor the Soviet Union but from the reluctance of the developed countries to increase their aid to the third world. The North-South dialogue of late 1970s and early 1980s is taking a fresh mode. It was stressed more in new global financial reforms and trade policies at Uruguay Round talks (1989), Rio-Earth summit meeting (1992).

The group of 77 is growing in magnitude and intensity. The group of 15 is a nuclear bloc within it working very powerfully. Recent G-15 meeting at Cyprus proves this.

"Also undeniably true is the fact that euphoria created by devastating consequences of 'Perestroika' and 'Glasnost' feet in the west has melted the capitalist soul of the US and its President seemed to be in a mellow mood? But will the US play the ball with economically backward and developing countries as willingly as he did with latest pal glory from Moscow."[15]

In the present world each and every system is in transition. Recent non-aligned meeting at Harare showed that its backbone is broken, after the failure to reach to a consensus among its members. Members of NAM disagreed over a number of issues. The dissolution of Yugoslavia—one of its founding members was a major factor for this. Pakistan also raised the Kashmir issue irritating India. Sri Lankan crisis is still unresolved. Some opine that after the receding and virtual collapse of the cold war, the non-aligned doctrine is losing its value and is redundant. But how will America gain from it is yet to be seen.

Now that democratic party has. come to power after twelve-years, changes in foreign policies strategy is excepted. Of course, President-elect Bill Clinton says, he has the same attitude to Middle-East like his predecessor. Yet Saddam Hussein is the man to congratulate him at the instance, he became elected. The New President announced friendly ties with India, a major democratic and leading champion of third world countries. It is yet to be seen what will be the US attitude to Pakistan and China.

Some predict that two superpowers were maintaining balance of power in the world. Now since the balance is upset, there is more danger for the world. The offence and egoism of the tiny nations will lead the world to disaster. Some also opine unified Germany and Japan will come to be superpowers and the US will recede to lower position.

Whether it will be a unipolar world or multipolar world depends not only on the US policies but also on so many other factors. It is yet to be seen how logistically the US would behave in such situations and how long it will perpetuate its commanding role in world politics. It is yet to be seen which hypothesis is leading us to conclusion.

NOTES

1. Angelli Enrico and Murphy Craig, *America's Quest for Supremacy and the Third World* (London, 1988).
2. See Deborah Larson, *The Origins of Containment* (Princeton, 1985), p. 323.
3. Michael J. Parenti, *The Anti-Communist Impulse* (New York: Random House, 1969), p. 261.
4. See Barnet, *Roots of War* (Baltimore: Penguin, 1972), p. 48.
5. See Stephen D. Kraussen, *Defending the National Interest: Raw Material Investment and U.S. Foreign Policy* (Princeton, 1978).
6. See Kees van der Pijl, *The Making of Atlantic Ruling Cases* (London, 1984).
7. Joseph Nye, "U.S. Power and Reagan Policy," *Orbis*, 26 (1982), pp. 319-412. Also see William Avery and David Rapkin, ed., *America in a Changing World Political Economy* (London: Longman, 1982).
8. George Liska "The Third World: Regional Systems and Global Order" in Robert Osgood et al, *Retreat from Empire* (Baltimore: John Hopkins Press, 1973), pp. 279-343.
9. Stephen Graubard, *Kissinger: Portrait of a Mind* (New York: Norton, 1977), p. 170.

10. Jeffrey A. Hart, *The New International Economic Order* (London: St. Martin's Press, 1984), pp. 103-42.
11. Annapurna Nautiyal, "The Changing Face of Soviet Union: Implications for India," *Third Concept* (May 1992), p. 23.
12. J.P. Sharma, "The Arab Summit: A Move Towards Pan-Arab Security," *Third Concept* (June 1990), pp. 8-9.
13. Rachana Chaitanya, "The New International Order," *Third Concept* (May 1992), p. 27.
14. Preetham Prakash, "Yen in International Trade," *Third Concept* (June 1989), pp. 43-44.
15. Padma Rao, "G-15 Summit: A Good Start," *Third Concept* (June 1990), pp. 9-11.

The End of the Cold War and American Foreign Policy: U.S. Policy vis-a-vis European Community Federalism

DIPANKAR BASU

Foreign policy is purposive and value judgments are its bases. However, a state must operate in a real world and values have no meaning except in concrete terms and in relation to specific situations. In short, values must be translated into objectives. But the formulation of realistic policy objective should be based upon a correct appraisal of the power potential of the nation. In other words, there should be an appropriate relationship between ends and means.

USA, like other nations and the individuals, face the world in a different way—its foreign policy depends on how the US reacts and sees the world and its place in it. How USA is to act in the international area, especially vis-a-vis the European Community depends to a large extent upon its geography, historical background and experience. National styles behind the US foreign policy depends upon situations, conditions and environment and the state system, in which the US coexist. The US's approach to international affairs is deeply rooted in and guided by a widely-shared consensus about the purpose of foreign policy, i.e. that the US government should reflect the American people's ideals to contribute to national security and international stability; to facilitate prosperity; and to promote freedom and democracy.

In general, the US has isolated itself from the European state system, as its national style was based on its domestic experiences and democratic values and outlook. Not schooled by continuous involvement in international politics, as were the Europeans, the US approach to foreign policy was peculiar in nature and different from that of other great powers.

During the most of the nineteenth century and the early twentieth century, the US was able to preserve its historical isolation from power politics and protect its security because the balance of power in Europe was maintained by Britain. The priority of internal political and economic tasks also demanded that the US isolate itself from European powers. Though America's entry into I World War was what made it possible to contain Germany's offensive of 1918, leading to German defeat, but the US wanted nothing to do with international politics.

The US began to play a decisive political role again only when the balance of European power was upset by the eruption of II World War in 1939. The US intervened mainly because defence of the US security always involved more than physical security and also that security of the democratic USA was interwoven with survival of other democracies specially that of France and Britain.

The expectation of a post-war "era of good feeling" between the US and the Soviet Union failed due to Soviet "Post-War expansion" and also due to other differences between the two great powers. The American sense of destiny or its ideas on depreciation of power politics so changed specially with the advent of cold war period.

The American commitment to a permanent role in international affairs, specially in Europe, may well be a dominant factor of post-World War II international affairs. It was a break for a nation that for a long time rejected any kind of "Alliances" and regarded the power politics of Europe to be a complete evil, which need to be avoided—but this idea changed during the post-II World War period and brought about changes—for the first time there was peace-time standing army with forces stationed in every hemisphere of the globe, including in Europe; secondly there were factors of secrecy and clandestinity out of harmony with the tradition and spirit of people. Over and above there was the phenomenon of large "limited wars" with much loss of American life, but no clear victory or defeat. Indeed there was the US's leadership with all its borders and all its glory.

As William Clayton, Under-Secretary of State for Economic Affairs of the USA, pointed out in November 1946, "Time and Science having mustered those physical phenomena which served as the chief bulwark of the isolationists, the American people are now settling down to their responsibilities as full partners in World Affairs and appear to like it."

With the announcement of Truman Doctrine on March 12, 1947, the US took a decision towards the strategy of containment—a policy of firmness, patience and recognition that Soviet Union was no longer just a difficult ally but an enemy. During the period of containment, the US policy was towards giving military assistance, as per the Brussels Pact of Collective Self-Defense, 1948, and establishment of NATO in 1949 and economic assistance through Marshall Plan, under European Economic Cooperation Act of 1948, to the West European countries.

During the period of policy of containment, the US made a quick shift to assuming the leadership of the West. In these years President Harry Truman along with his first secretary of state General Marshall and later on with Dean Ackeson reconstructed a prosperous and democratic Western Europe, and made the nations away from their past rivalries towards cooperation and unity. The US also created West Germany and admitted it into the Western community and provided Europe with security. This alliance of Western Europe and the US has survived more than four decades and has been a key reason for the avoidance of nuclear war.

II World War in Europe had devastated the economy of all countries, both winners and losers alike. There was a fear that the Soviet Union would be able to exploit Europe's post-War economic and psychological vulnerability.

A collapse of Europe posed again the fundamental question as to whether Europe was vital to the US security. Europe's vital importance became clear to USA in the emerging bi-polar world—because of its enormous potential and its geographic position, Europe's security was indeed inseparable from the US security. European Economic Recovery was also essential for the US to prevent the Soviet Union to control the Western approach to the Atlantic. America was mindful of the advantage which the US has enjoyed through the existence of a large scale domestic market with no internal trade barriers and believed that similar advantages can accrue to the European countries.

In 1948, Marshall Plan was passed by the Congress. American Aid was also conditional on a basis of economic cooperation between European states. Economic Cooperation Act of 1948 called specially for European Economic Integration.

So the US officials declared that European Integration was the prerequisite for Europe's recovery and the necessary basis for long range prosperity. The American aim was to modernize the industrial machinery to overcome the cartelization of industry and the inefficiency of small family enterprises (as in France) and to eliminate divisions among the nations. Europe's industries were expected to enlarge and become competitive by the creation of a United States of Europe.

The aim of Marshall Plan was to have economic cooperation, specially between the Western European Nations and also between them and USA; and to have a plan for common needs and common recovery with the US providing funds and the Europeans to assume initiative in the matters of planning. The result was also reflected in the establishment of Organization for European Economic Cooperation, to be administered by the European Cooperative Administration. Originally USA intended all the nations of Europe, including the USSR and the Eastern

Europe to plan joint recovery—as otherwise USA would have been blamed for division of Europe and intensification of cold war. But the Soviet Union and East Europe never participated.

Soon after Marshall Plan was launched, it was realized that Europe's economic recovery was impossible in an atmosphere of tension and insecurity, as prevalent in Europe during that time.

In 1947, France and Britain signed Treaty of Dunkirk for mutual defense against threat to their security. In 1948, Great Britain, France and the Benelux countries signed Brussel Pact of Collective Self-Defence, as a counterpart of OEEC, for military cooperation. Just as the success of OEEC has depended upon the influx of American capital, the Brussels Pact members also expected their alliance to attract American support—they were not disappointed as NATO was established in 1949, with USA, UK, France, Canada, Denmark, Iceland, Italy, Norway, Portugal and the Benelux. For the first time, USA committed itself to an alliance in peace time.

To USA, Europe became "our first line of defence." America would fight to prevent the Soviet attack. Instead of allowing Balance of Power to be disturbed and being once more drawn into a war after it started, the US now expected to prevent this by committing itself to preserve the balance in peace time also. The presumption was that fear of meeting American resistance and fighting an all-out war with the US would deter a potential aggressor.

A policy of deterrence mainly relied on American Superior Air-Power and a Forward strategy that is European Defence to be built at the so-called inter-German border. The US's help also allowed the revival of Germany's economic recovery and NATO provided military security—but the Soviet Union reacted to West Germany's growing autonomy by blockading West Berlin in 1948. The US helped Germany in Berlin Airlift and demonstrated its determination to hold Europe and not to allow further Soviet expansion.

Ironically it was the renewed fear of Germany's rising strength that stimulated West European Nation's efforts toward European integration. "Fully Revived Germany" struck fear into the minds of most of Germany's neighbours. Germany's recovery mainly helped by the US's response to the cold war, posed a serious problem for Germany's rearmament. How could they hold Germany in check when it was potentially the strongest nation in Europe outside the Soviet Union? It was then realized that only through the creation of a super-national community, to which Germany could transfer certain sovereign rights, that German power could be controlled. France took the initiative and aimed toward this goal—this approach stressed super-national cooperation and institutions within a limited sphere and the creation of common interest within that particular area of activity before extending it to other fields.

So the European Economic Community was established in 1958, with six countries (France, West Germany, Italy and Belgium, Netherlands, Luxembourg), with an aim to include other countries as members, in the near future. However, in 1963, France's President Charles de Gaulle vetoed Britain's entry into the EEC. In 1966, France also withdrew from NATO's integrated command structure, though remaining a member of the alliance.

It was only in 1972, that after various conferences and negotiations, Britain, Denmark and Iceland joined EEC, increasing its members to nine countries – Spain and Portugal joined the EEC only in 1986; later on Greece joined EEC increasing the number of members to twelve.

In between, the war in Vietnam left the US disillusioned with anti-Communism as a rationale for American global involvement – the question was also where could America draw "Frontiers." So there was a shift from "Ideal Politik" to "Real Politik," from cold war to Detente. The question was also how to conduct foreign policy without a consensus, a situation seen specially during Nixon's regime from January 1969 to 1974 (till Nixon resigned) and during Ford's Administration till January 1976, when Mr. Jimmy Carter became the President of USA – Carter was in favour of interdependent world. But Detente collapsed with Soviet invasion of Afghanistan in 1979 and as such there was a search for consensus and recognition of Human Rights.

American leaders have long considered the dominance of Europe, by it, as essential for its economic and military security. But in the era of Detente, NATO developed cracks as the US dealt directly with the Soviet Union – as such not surprisingly European states also went on their own and economic issues proved divisive within Atlantic Community. It is also that during Reagan and Bush Administration, economic relations and other matters, between USA and the European Community members were at odds.

At the height of cold war, there was the rivalry between democracy and totalitarianism; but at the end of cold war, another form of competition has been emerging; that is a contest between forces of integration and fragmentation in the contemporary international environment – integration happening in the fields of communication, revolution, economics, security, integration of ideas, and in the field of international peace and security.

There are also forces of "Fragmentation" at work that are resurrecting old barriers between nations and peoples – like the disintegrating forces of Nationalism, in the field of economics, where they manifest themselves as "Protectionism": (that is effort by various means to isolate individual economies from the working of world market forces), racial tension that can develop both among states and within them; in the area of religion; and others like drug problem, Aids epidemic, ecological problems, global warming, environmental pollution, population pressure, emigration problems, breakdown of education system, linguistic anxieties, and regional rivalries.

In brief, the problems in the post-cold war world are more likely to arise from competing processes—Integration versus Fragmentation—than from the kinds of competing ideological visions that dominated the cold war.

The new geo-political cartography provides no immediate answer to the question of which of these processes might most threaten the future security interests of the US. In this context consider the future of Europe. The reunification of Germany, break-up of the USSR, collapse of Communism in the East European countries, rise of nationalism in Yugoslavia and Czechoslovakia, and other places of Europe, Basque problem in Spain, the Irish question, the rivalry between the Flemings and Walloons in Belgium—all these are bringing about realignments of political, military and economic power in modern history. It has come about largely as a result of those integrative forces that brought out an end to cold war—that is the triumph of democratic politics and market economics. It can also be said that this victory for liberalism in Europe is producing both integrative and disintegrative consequences. In Germany, demands for Self-Determination have brought about political integration, but at the same time economic efforts could be disintegrative. There are also concerns as to whether the progress the European Community (EC) has made towards removing trade and immigration barriers will be sufficient to tie the United Germany firmly to the West or whether the present Germany will build its own center of power further to the east, thus destroying the spirit of Maastricht Treaty, which was signed in December 1991, at Maastricht in Holland, by EC members, a Monetary Union, Political Union, Federaliam, Joint Foreign Affairs and common Defence policy.

The Maastricht Treaty requires approval by each of the twelve EC members—so far not ratified by all—and promises that a European citizen can live, work, vote anywhere; free movement of goods across borders; higher living standards in poorer nations; standard working conditions. It also envisages a creation of European Monetary Institute by 1.1.94, and Euro-Central Bank by 1.1.97 and also coordinate economic and monetary policies and to have a European Currency Unit replacing national currencies. Secondly, it stresses for a political union by bringing social, industrial affairs, health, education, trade, environment, energy, culture, tourism, consumer and civil protection under EC's jurisdiction. Thirdly, there is a proposal for a unified foreign policy with majority voting on specific actions. Fourthly, it envisages a Common Joint Defence policy. Fifthly, it has proposed that 518 member Assembly or European Parliament should finally share the right to make Community law with the nations. Lastly, the Maastricht proposals call for a "Federal Goal" for the new union, eventually going beyond what is now envisaged.

However, the latest news with regards to the Maastricht Treaty is that EC members are divided on European Political Union. There are conflicts between the "Euroskeptcis" and the "Europhobes"– there is also a tension between Eurocracy, having about 12,000 people, with its headquarter at Brussels and the others who are against it. Britain and Denmark oppose deciding some foreign policy questions by majority vote rather than by consensus, Portugal and the Netherlands share British wariness about a Common Defence Policy (the reason for which Sweden, Switzerland, Finland and Austria have not been yet welcomed, unless they give affirmative to join the common Defence strategy also). Britain has also opposed to extend EC's control over workers' right and other labour issues; Spain demands rich partners to help the poorer. Britain also wants any reference to a "Federal goal" for political union deleted as it interprets the phrase as reaching to a "superstate" with a strong federal government.

Recently tensions have also arisen regarding the Exchange Rate Mechanism, which has brought about a near collapse of Britain's and Italy's banking system.

The question is also with regards to "where is the perfect European?"–Is it that the perfect European should be technical as a Portuguese! Humble as a Spaniard! Cool king like a British! Available as a Belgian! Controlled as an Italian! Driving like the French! Organized as a Greek! Famous as a Luxembourger! Discreet as a Dane! Generous as a Dutchman! Humorous as a German! Sober as the Irish! The result of an analysis made to this extent by a Media Sales organization in Brussels found that "the average European does not exist!"

The expansion of Soviet and American influence over Europe at the end of World War II had effect of a glacier–it froze things in place, thereby controlling old rivalries and bringing peace (even of a "cold" peace) to a continent that had known little of it throughout its history.

But now that the cold war is over, geopolitical glaciers are retreating, the situation is becoming fluid once again, and certain familiar features of the European landscape are once again coming into view–that is a strong German state, together with ethnic and religious antagonisms among Germany's neighbours to the East. Is the history repeating itself?

End of cold war period can be parallel with the decades between the two World Wars—collapse of an empire in the East; rise of jealous nationalities, economic upheaval; mass flights of the people, and Germans' attacks on foreigners, as also others. Of course it can be said that though the West is confronted with serious problems, still they are not as catastrophic as they were between the two World Wars. The question is: Would the West, after four decades of starring down a nuclear gun barrel, would slip into an era of democratic good feeling and effortless property, secure in the knowledge that it had won the ideological war? Or, can we say that the greater issue that has emerged is the specter of W.H. Auden's 1939 vision reborn:

In the nightmare of dark,
All the dogs of Europe bark,
And the living Nations wait,
Each sequestered in its hate.

In the year 1992, the Europe is rattled with a message of danger—a danger that brave new Europe of emancipated peoples, vanishing borders, and resurgent democracy is reverting to an older and cruder form.

Age of complacency about Europe's future is crushing around EC members. National electorates are notably challenging all the conventional assumptions about the EC, but at the same time the community itself is neglecting the political and economic traumas that "are rocking the newly de-communized nations. Old varieties are crumbling, even in France, the homeland of Jean Monet, the European Community's founding visionary. Since the 1990s, French have voiced suspicions about Germany's rearmament and economic dominance.

Under the circumstances, the question is: can the US retreat into a kind of new isolationism? European officials are faced with Yugoslavia's problems—is it a "quarrel in a far away country between people of whom we know nothing" as Chamberlain said in 1938, regarding Hitler's grab for Czechoslovakia?

Think of what secretary of state George Marshall, in his formal speech at Harvard University announcing the Marshall Plan, said: "But to my mind it is of vast importance to our people to reach some general understanding rather than to react to the passions and prejudices of the moment. We are too remote from all these countries to grasp at all the real significance . . . and yet the whole world's future hangs on proper judgment, hangs on a realization by the American people of what can best be done, of what might be done."

It can be said that resemblances to the inter-war period may be there, but Western Europe is such a vastly transformed landscape that any reprieve of old-fashioned great power conflicts is unlikely. Alternatives to the European Community that is Fascism and Communism are thoroughly discredited, mainly because of the fact that social safety nets are secure more than before. The increase of Bundesbank interest rates in September 1992, have had a serious effect on the economies of other EC nations—Sterling's sudden withdrawal from Exchange Rate Mechanism is a fact of concern. A currency storm blows European unity of course.

To the US strategist currency crisis was not just about money but revealed the political sclerosis at the heart of attempts to forge a united Europe. The turmoil in the currency market of Europe recently also mirrored widespread anxiety over the political and economic future of the EC. The question is also whether Maastricht Treaty can survive? There is no doubt that a lack of economic cohesion within the EC exists. Suddenly the EC members are having a doubt about pan-European projects and dreams that beckoned so much in the aftermath of cold war and collapse of Communism.

In the face of unpreparedness in the EC to go forward with monetary and political union, it is to be seen how US foreign policy adjusts to this. It is also to be noted as Paul Goble, one of the foremost American foreign policy experts, says: "The world is not going to settle down into a new steady state. If you act as if it is, you are dead."

In the winter of 1990-91, the US administrative officials continued to downplay the extent of the Soviet Union's economic difficulties. West Europeans by contrast saw the issue as one of geopolitics rather than economic deficiency. The EC was willing to help the Soviet Union and several EC members notably Germany, France and Spain have moved on their own to assist Moscow economically. The US administration has avoided a conflict with the West European by not objecting to these economic aid efforts. However, until recently Washington equivocated on the issue of whether it would move from neutrality to a more active stance. The US administration seemed to be acting less out of conviction than from a desire not to be isolated from Germany and EC policy on this issue. In short, Washington is yet to settle down on a long range policy.

The most serious problems of the US as it faces the future are the lack of foreign policy consensus and the question of whether the American people still want to play an active and energetic role in the world. A people and their government should share the responsibility for wise decisions and policy to be made by a truly representative government and implemented by professionals of high character – whenever this has been done, the foreign policy of US been a force for good in the world and America's precious liberty have been secure.

The conventional view of the Congressional role in American foreign policy making has long been that Congress is a minor actor at best. The Congressional role is to follow the President's lead – if that pattern has changed at all, it is presumed to have been as a result of the unpopularity of Vietnam war.

Two political parties have flip-flopped. The Republicans appear to be interventionist in foreign policy and Democrats are much less willing to intervene abroad, to use force or the threat of force to support foreign policy objections. Both Bush and Clinton are "Internationalist" and they would like to show, if necessary, "the supremacy of the US" – both are not "Ideologue."

The absence of genuine consensus on foreign policy is the deteriorating condition of the US economy, as economic power, like military power has diffused in the state system – money being always treated as an important factor of international politics.

Recent EC-US Trade War over farm subsidies is a pointer to this extent. With Ms. Carla Hallis, US Trade representative, announcing on 5 November 1992, a 200 percent stiff duties on EC wines and food exports, the fragile unity of the EC has all but collapsed. The US has also released an additional list of 17 billion worth of EC industrial products on which the US may impose tariffs unless the dispute is resolved.

In economic terms the US demand that Brussels give a firm commitment to freeing agricultural trade and drop its practice of giving generous hand outs to farmers makes perfect sense. In political terms, however, it shifts the lion's share of pain of adjustment to Europe.

However, on November 20, 1992, the US and its EC trading partners reached a sweeping agreement in farm subsidies that averted a transatlantic trade war and cleared the way for a global deal to reduce barriers to commerce – in spite of the immediate objections of France. This agreement still requires the approval of 12 EC members, and later on to be approved by GATT negotiations in Geneva for approval by the 108 nations involved. Economists estimate that a general agreement on tariffs and trade world deal could pump as much as $ 200 billion in the weak global economy. In this connection it is to be noted that a unified EC would create the biggest consumer market in the world – in 1990, population in EC was 343.5 millions compared to the US's 251.1 millions, and gross domestic product in 1990 in EC was $ 6,015 billions, compared to the US's $ 5,392 billions.

Both Mr. Bush and the US President-elect Mr. Clinton have said that the successful conclusion of the world trade talks is a top foreign policy objective. However, Mr. Clinton was guarded about the deal saying that "I am hopeful, but we have got to look at it." One of Clinton's aides, Mr. George Stephano Poulos said, "If foreign countries won't open their markets, we have to get tough."

We also find that France and Britain were locked in a new row over the Maastricht Treaty after French President Mr. Francois Mitterand lashed out at Prime Minister Mr. John Major, for postponing British ratification of European Union. It is so that new entry in the EC would be possible only after EC had settled its budgetary wrangles in December 1992 and when the 12 EC members had ratified Maastricht Treaty.

Britain also wants the EC not to become a "Defence Club"—she is so willing to have new members like Sweden, Switzerland, Austria, Finland—if not others—who would also like to be neutral. But France and Germany support the EC's demand on assurances on "Defense matters" and would not like to see members remaining neutral in Defence policy. Are the EC members willing to give binding assurances? No one knows what the common Defence policies would be and how far they would the US defence strategy both in Europe and in other places of the world. What will happen then to NATO also?

It is to be seen also how far the EC's objectives of a Monetary Union or Political Union or Common Foreign Affairs and Federal goal affect the US in every aspect—both in the domestic and international fields.

In the face of Maastricht Treaty being challenged both by the European politicians and the people on the ground of doubt about its viability and stability, can the US retreat again into a kind of neo-isolationism?

We find that the chief purpose of American foreign policy vis-a- vis European Community is the security of democratic America; the balance of power, however defined and whatever its military ingredients, is not an end in itself, but the means to preserve security. Successive administrations in USA had felt that this end required the maintenance of international environment congenial to the survival of democratic societies. The fundamental orientation of American foreign policy, therefore, has been to support the democracies, old and new in Western Europe.

The basic and critical question for the future stability of Europe is the extent to which the cold war glacier permanently altered the terrain it covered so long. Integrationist structures like the EC and NATO suggest such alteration, but they could also have been artifacts of the glaciation itself. If so, these organizations will become increasingly vulnerable as the forces of fragmentation revive.

No economic and security structure for Europe can hope to be viable over the long term unless it incorporates and gives benefits to all the major states of Europe. The classic lesson is that of the Treaty of Versailles of 1919, which sought to build peace, without Germany and the Soviet Union.

But neither the EC nor NATO has given sufficient attention as to how each might restructure itself to accommodate the interests of the former Warshaw Pact states, including the newly-independent states of the previous Soviet Union. Few efforts have been made to think how the EC can expand its scope of activities to counter the fragmentationist challenges coming from the reunification of Germany, the liberation of Eastern Europe and the collapse of the USSR.

Critics observe that the US has used its influence over the years to favour "Integration" over "Fragmentation" in Europe—without that influence, it is difficult to see how integration in the EC could have proceeded as far as it has..

But the Americans cannot expect to maintain the authority the cold war gave them on Europe, for very much longer, especially with the disintegration of the USSR. It is so required that the US should consider what new or modified integrative structures might replace that the US played in "freezing" disintegrative forces in Europe during the cold war period otherwise serious imbalances could develop in that part of the world as well.

It is said that after the recent Exchange Rate Mechanism debacle in Western Europe, the grand vision of Federal Europe is an illusion. What then does Europe do?

It has been suggested that the best thing for Europe is to do "Free Trade." With the EC's single market project there will be free flow capital, goods and labour within the twelve—widening of this single market, first to the Eastern Europe and neighbours, and then boldly to the West: the North America, will be the best policy.

But with the visions of a Federal Europe fading, there can be a cooperation between Europe and America. The US is afraid that a fortress Europe will shut its trade doors. Europe is also worried about the North American Free Trade Agreement, which would be creating a trading zone demographically larger than the EC.

A transatlantic free trade area merging the two would not only prevent a trade war and increase prosperity on the both but also have a global effect. Europe and North America together account for more than half of world GNP—in case of trade merger between the EC and USA, they would dictate the terms of the world economy; it could also dictate a world of free trade where Japan might find itself shut out of the new world economic order, if it had thoughts of creating a rival Asian bloc or if it refuses to modify its drive for market dominance.

Almost fifty years ago, Churchill in his "Iron Curtain Speech" gave a call for a "fraternal association of the English-speaking peoples, an association so close between America and British Empire that "eventually there may come the principle of common citizenship."

President Harry Truman responded with a looser but wider idea, an alliance not just with Britain but with all of Western Europe. The result was NATO – America's first ever peace time alliance.

At present there is again a need for alliance, not military this time but economic. The threat is not the Soviet Empire but growing economic nationalism and protectionism that appears to be threatening fifty years of unparalleled world prosperity. To this, the answer may be a transatlantic pact, a free-trade zone embracing all like-minded, market-oriented, democratic peoples, from Vancouver to Vladivostik. Political Union may be left for the future – may be then the engine of nationalism shall be at a stop. The aim for tomorrow appears to be "utopia"; whereas a modest goal for today is a "Transatlantic Free Trade Zone." It is expected that President-elect Bill Clinton will take a bold step towards this extent, with a spirit of cooperation with the Economic Community – this can only bring about an "Integration" and not "Fragmentation."

Rethinking the Superness of American Power

MANOJ SONI

We are living in an age of paradoxes, unnerving yet indispensable. No century has witnessed rate and scope of technological and scientific expansion for the betterment of life as ours. But at the same time, it is our century which has produced not only means but also socially-institutionalized will to shrink our planet into a vast crematory. There are innumerable illustrations of these examples of often bewildering paradoxes in which all nations small and great have their contributions. And as such, the United States is no exception.

Yet, so penetrative and expansive has been the American influence in the matters of life and death of many a nation that the twentieth century has been called "the American century."[1] Now, as this century is unfolding its last decade, it may also unravel the mystery as to whom belongs the next century? Though we have no intention to indulge in prophecy, yet the astonishing pace of international events has certainly created so complex a scenario that the greatest of nations will increasingly find itself enfeebled to control, manage and resolve crises after crises destabilizing the interstate order.

A crisis is a situation in which the restitutive mechanisms of the system are no longer functioning well and therefore, the system is poised either for transformation or disintegration. The history of international relations has proved this well beyond doubt from the earliest days of inter-societal exchange relationship on organized basis, to the breakdown of the fedual and balance of power mechanisms, to the present disruption in the bipolar configuration of international power relationships hinging heavily on the nuclear deterrence mechanisms. On the one hand, the thaw in the mutually rivaling super power relations, the actual and significant de-escalation in militarisation and global arms race and the apparent ending of the cold war do raise hopes for not only tomorrow but a better tomorrow, yet on the other hand, there have arisen severe interpellations which have enfeebled the restitutive mechanisms of the interstate order.

Although these interpellations are far beyond the wills and controls of nation states, the external behaviour of such a great and powerful nation like the United States is bound to play a determining role with regard to the emerging international system, as it is influenced and counter-influences these interpellations. This paper attempts to understand the post-cold war American foreign policy, as it is the period which has created an international social space of the interpellations to ground, and render an immediate address to them indispensable.

A) International Systemic Environment

In the immediate aftermath of II World War the international systemic environment distinctly reflected a state of intense conflict and mutually destructive rivalry between the United States and the Soviet Union. An acute stratification of the world in terms of power and resources culminating into nuclear bi-polarity, the resurfacing of incipient power vacuum in Asia, Africa, and Latin America, and a world-wide strategic encapsulation of weak states were some of the most devouring systemic phenomena capable of irreversible wrecking a precarious balance of terror.

With time, as revolutionary militancy waned, generation succeeded generation, and the economic and social development worked their way out, radical changes came about in the Soviet policy. The new Soviet thinking clearly revealed by Gorbachev in his Perestroika strived to moderate, and perhaps eliminate its distinctive 'Communist' natures: "For all the contradictions of the present day world, for all the diversity of social and political system in it, and for all the different choices made by the nations in different times, this world is nevertheless one whole. We are all passengers aboard one ship, the Earth, and we must not allow it to be wercked. There will be no second Noah's Ark."[2]

With remarkable swiftness there came about a substantial change in the official Soviet position regarding three important aspects of international politics: first, the political content of international relations which had traditionally been for Soviet an arena of conflict between the forces of socialism and progress and the forces of imperialism and reaction was modified. Gorbachev deliberately cast doubt on the Leninist conception of imperialism and raised the possibility that in the world system of the late twentieth century advanced capitalism would no longer be synonymous with militarism, aggressiveness and ruthless exploitation of poorer societies.[3] There has been a further shift away from Stalin's conception of 'two camps' in international relations. The Soviet leadership emphasized growing multipolarity in world politics and declared its refusal to view events solely 'through the prison of super power relations.'[4]

Second was a substantial change regarding ways of guaranteering national security. At the twenty seventh CPSU congress in 1985, Gorbachev dissociated himself from his party's traditional overwhelming reliance on military strength, when he declared that in the nuclear age the only reliable guarantees of national security are political ones.

And last but not the least has been a sea-change in the Soviet modes of participation in international economic life. The increasing interdependence of the contemporary world to which Gorbachev refers is most obvious in economic relations. Here the Soviet leaders spoke less of prospect of defeating the crisis-ridden West and more of drawing the leading powers into a new system of international regulation capable of ensuring universal economic stability and security.

Thus, from the mid-80s a fundamental shift is discernible in the international systemic environment from one of being conflict ridden and competitive to one being gradually transmitting itself apparently into co-existive and co-operative. It has lately been acknowledged that there are important areas in which collaboration and compromise can benefit both the sides. Although it is an exaggeration to say that the particularity of this pattern of behaviour particularly after the disintegration of the Soviet empire promises to have far-reaching implications for a future world order, it is also conceivable that this detente, if could not be channeled to serve the planet earth, can instead confront it with adverse consequences. For, the detente has not necessarily placed man on more assured world order, of even to a more assured peace, as some of us today may be inclined to believe.[5]

Echoing the argument Richard Nixon had warned the West against the overwhelm of Soviet Perestroika and Glasnost, which is now more relevant after the fall of the Soviet Union. "Those who parrot today," he confutes, "a fashionable slogan—'the cold war is over' trivialize the problems of Western Security."[6]

The US has to recognize that the situation it faces now is infinitely more complex than the one it faced at the outset of the cold war forty years ago. In addition to the systemic interpellations at a time when the CIS's superiority in conventional military forces and an accurate land based ICBMs is larger than ever before, the US and the west cannot counter the "peace offensive" simply by loudly proclaiming a cold war victory. Instead, the US must launch its own political offensive to achieve its strategic and geopolitical objectives.

On the other hand it would be naive to underestimate or ignore the CIS might. Gorbachev's assertions about the Soviet might are equally relevant with regard to the CIS as well. He had said, "If the Soviet Union, when it was much weaker than now, was in a position to meet all the challenges that it faced, then only a blind person would be unable to see that our capacity to maintain strong defenses [may be read also as strong offensives] and simultaneously resolve social and other tasks has enormously increased."[7] Also, the US is facing the daunting challenges posed by depolarisation of international power configuration and emergence of multiple poles of power with different currencies of power.

B) Domestic Environment

The second important aspect which influences the nature of a state's foreign policy is its domestic environment.

Governments invariably have to operate under restraints which derive from the domestic environment. The quality of capabilities that can be employed as an instrument of persuasion, inducement, or coercion act as restraint. The more overriding determinants arising out of domestic environment constitute socio-political-economic value system and talent, personality and scope of leadership.[8]

During more than four decades since 1945, while the socio- political value system has been stable, the economic power of the United States has eroded in relative (not necessarily absolute) terms. A variety of means exists for measuring this decline. Consider for example, the United States' share of the world's industrial production. In 1953, this stood at a level of 44.7 percent. Since that time it has steadily declined as shown in the table.[9]

Percentage Share of World Manufacturing Production

Year	USA	Japan	Third World
1953	44.7	2.9	6.5
1963	35.1	5.1	8.5
1973	33.0	8.8	9.9
1980	31.5	9.1	12.0

While many of the causes for the relative erosion in America's power position have been external, which we shall discuss in the next section, there have been internal causes as well. In explaining long-term causes of this relative decline, Robert Gilpin has drawn comparisons from the historical experiences of Athens, Rome, Holland, Britain, and the US. Gilpin formulates propositions to explain these cycles of decline.[10] In particular he finds the causes to lie in three key areas: external burdens of leadership, tendencies towards rising domestic consumption, and the international diffusion of technology.

Applied to the experience of the US, the impact of these can be readily identified. First, the initial costs of containment of the Soviet Union and then the globalisation of containment. The US spent an average of 7.4% of GDP on defense during 1960 and 1970 in contrast with West Germany's 3.9% and Japan's 0.9%.

Second, a pattern of increasing domestic consumption is also evident.[11] Moreover, the pattern of increasing consumption in relation to investment tended to accelerate during the first half of the 1980s, with some 3% of GDP represented by international borrowing to finance domestic consumption.

Third, the diffusion of American technology has proceeded on a global basis. Many newly industrialized countries have emerged as fierce economic competitors in their own right, rapidly moving from primary products into semi-manufactured goods, then into basic industries and subsequently into more sophisticated products.

The US is a great and wealthy nation with enormous natural assets as well as a vital and free political system. However, as everyone knows, balance sheet consists of both asset and liabilities and those of the US are growing at a fearsome rate. If those liabilities created by failure of domestic economic policy are not corrected in near future, they might cost the US its pre-eminent roles as a world power. And this is essentially what the new Clinton administration is currently pre-occupied with. And it is the direction and results of this occupation that will provide answers or make America mute to the emergent global challenges in the post-cold war era.

C) Total National Capability

One of the most important and yet one of the most difficult tasks for the practitioner of international policies deals with is the analysis of the capability of states to formulate and implement their policy objectives. As Harold and Margaret Sprout say: "With reference to historical cases, the analysis is designed to answer the question: how was it possible for a given state to exert an influence or to play a role?"[12]

Among the more deterministic theories of national power, few have experienced a more seductive and persistent appeal than geography. Until half a century ago geographical position to national power appeared to be one of the most stable and predictable factors in international politics.

Another important foreign policy input is the cluster of socio- political factors. The social structure of a society and the changes that it undergoes are crucial determinants of the degree of internal conflict and harmony within a society, of the groups from which political factors are recruited, of the extent to which the human resources of the society are developed, of its capability to adjust to change—all factors that can in turn change the contents and effectiveness of a state's action abroad.

The recent outbreak of hostilities in the West Asia bears testimony to Claustewitz's famous aphorism that "War is nothing but continuation of political relationship by other means." Claustewitz writes in an age when the concept of limited war was rooted in the temper and technology of the times. And now when man has added to his arsenals weapons of mass destruction, war is still contemplatable and actually fought as viable alternative in the pursuit of political objectives.

States have arrived at such a deadlock in their search for security that peace seems to depend on the degree to which the rival states can maintain the so-called balance of terror with their respective military might. And this might plays a crucial role in the formulation and implementation of a state's external behaviour.

Since the end of the second world war, the United States has successfully managed to control all the above factors of national capability to serve its foreign policy objectives. The galloping technology and telescoping communications have tended to make this world a global town. There has been a generally well-maintained stability in the American socio-political system with a very few exceptions. And in the military sphere the US has been consistently enhancing and strengthening its position as a super power.

But, for today's America the focus is gradually shifting from these factors of national capability to matters of economic growth and development. Today one may well ask whether relations among nations are not characterized by a permanent shift toward goals of economic welfare and a concomitant rise of importance of economic resources and economic instrument in inter-state competitions. Such a change is also linked to reduction in power rivalry and widespread, if not yet universal, internal political liberalization.

We may see changes in the international economy not as providing a resolution to age-old problems of conflict, but as intimately tied to that conflict. The ever-changing economic features of nation states affect their strategic position as well as their perception of national security.

The US emerged from World War II as the pre-eminent military and economic power in the non-communist world. Contemporary scholarship on international relations has increasingly adopted the term hegemony to describe the position of the US during this immediate post-war period,[13] although other students of the subject have preferred the term leadership.[14] But two sea changes have unmistakably been clear in the late

1980s which could rob America of its hegemonic pre-eminence in international relations.

First, the rise of Japan has been an almost continuous process since the proclamation of the "Japanese Miracle" in the early 1960s. In the decade of eighties that began with the publication of "Japan as Number One,"[15] Japan's economic march expanded into high technology industrial sector and international finance, an expansion that fundamentally changed its bilateral relationship with the United States.

As Reagan Administration's strategy of fiscal expansion produced massive American borrowing abroad, it became clear that Japan was home to the largest pool of exportable capital in the world economy. The necessity to finance part of the US budget deficit with foreign banks, the necessity over the last four years for foreign banks to acquire more than 150 billion dollars to support the US currency, the US trade deficit and growing foreign debt – all these factors and more have eroded America's economic pre-eminence, especially in the post-cold war era.

The second most probable challenge to American dominance could come from a united European Community. The European Community, if it becomes politically cohesive, would have the population, resources, economic wealth, technology, and actual and potential military strength to be the pre-eminent power of the twenty-first century. Japan, the US and the Soviet Union have specialized respectively in investment, consumption and arms. Europe balances all the three. It invests less of its GNP than Japan but more than the US and the Soviet Union. It consumes less of its GNP than the US but more than Japan and the Soviet Union. It arms less than the US and the Soviet Union but more than Japan.[16]

It is also quite possible to conceive of a European ideological appeal comparable to the American one. Throughout the world, people line up at the American consulates seeking immigration visas. In Brussels, countries line up at the door of the community seeking admission. A federation of democratic, wealthy, socially diverse, mixed economy societies could be a powerful force on the world scene.

Hence, in any collaborative initiative that is undertaken the US faces a final choice – the claims of leadership that it will make and price that it is willing to pay for those claims. Japan has now become the largest donor of foreign aid. The Bush Administration had signaled its willingness to have the EC lead in organizing economic assistance for eastern Europe. The American fiscal deadlock has made it difficult for the US to lead on issues of international economic importance. If the threat of CIS and Muslim fundamentalist military powers recedes, then a central question will be, what price the US and its tax payers are willing to pay in order to play central role in sustaining an altered international economic order.

(d) Foreign Policy Objectives and Strategies

The prime foreign policy objective of any super power, or for that of any sovereign independent state is invariably of controlling international and domestic environment. As far as the control and manipulation of international systemic environment in terms of the politico-ideological and strategic issues is concerned the US has managed it successfully, especially in the post-cold war era.

But, now a fundamental shift in the US foreign policy objectives and strategy is becoming evident. The identification of economic competition in the world market place among advanced capitalist countries completely overshadows east-west politico-ideological issues. Since the economic shock of the 1970s, some observers have predicted a world economy divided into regional blocs; the consolidation of Europe and the rise of Japan are pointers in that direction.

By the end of the 1980s momentum has been building up within the US and dominant sectors of the ruling class for an economic confrontation with Japan. Yet this resentment at Japanese ascendancy is compered by a recognition of the US dependency on Japanese financing or the US deficit and supplies of essentials.

The second major area for the post-cold war American Foreign Policy objectives and strategy to deal with is Western Europe, particularly the EEC countries. The EEC has been accumulating huge trade surpluses with the US. Over a good part of the 1980s amounting to over 20 billion dollars in 1987. The US spends more on NATO than the 15 members together: their expenditures amount to 60 percent of the US military budget. As one Congress person summarized the US relation to Europe: "American tax dollars are spent to defend our allies who use what they save to clobber us in trade wars."[18] The rise of Europe as an economic super power, and the growing relative importance of Europe as an economic super power, and the growing relative importance of economic market power as the basis for global influence will certainly be a plentyous might of the twenty-first century.

Given the apparent symptoms of relative American power erosion in the last decade of the 20th century, if the next century is not the American century it is most likely to be the European century. The nation of world leadership that passed westward across the atlantic in the early twentieth century could move back eastward a hundred years later.

After all as Rousseau aphorised, "If Sparta and Rome perished, what state can hope to endure forever?"[19]

Post Script

Throughout this paper a major recent international event concerning the United states has not been discussed. It is the Gulf war between Iraq and the coalition of 28 countries led by the US.

It has been a foregone conclusion ever since the US opted to put its Super Power might on the side of occupied Kuwait that Iraq will either be forced to back off, or would incur heavy cost if it remains adamant on a military solution. Expectedly Iraq chose the latter and faced horrible consequences of that choice which was, nevertheless, based on a number of viable strategic and psychological deterrents.

On the other hand, although the US has won the war, it has yet to win peace. President Bush recognized this in his ceasefire address to the nation when he cautioned, "We must now begin to look beyond victory and war. We must meet the challenge of peace."

And given the imperative of the systemic interpellations and relative decline of the Superness of the American power and given the extremely complex and unstable West Asian power equations, the president seems right in summarizing American role as "a catalyst for (hot) peace."

NOTES

1. For a detailed note on these interpellations, see Manoj Soni, "Imperatives of the Post-Cold War Era," *The Third Concept*, July 1992, pp. 31-32.
2. Mikhail Gorbachev, *Perestroika: The New Thinking for Our Country and the World* (New York: Harper and Row, 1987), p. 12.
3. Neil Malcolm, "De-Stalinization and Soviet Foreign Policy: The Roots of New Thinking," in Tsuyoshi Hasegawa and Alex Pravada, eds., *Perestroika: Soviet Domestic and Foreign Policies* (New Delhi: Sage, 1990), p. 195.
4. Mikhail Gorbachev, pp. 117, 212-13.
5. For a conceptual analysis of Super power Detente, see A.P. Rana, "Detente and Non Alignment: A Conceptual Study," *International Studies*, October 1974, pp. 752-74.
6. Richard Nixon, "American Foreign Policy: The Bush Agenda," *Foreign Affairs,* 1988/89, pp. 204-5.

7. Mikhail Gorbachev, p. 220.
8. See especially Graham H. Shepard, "Personality Effects on American Foreign Policy, 1969-84," *International Studies Quarterly*, Vol. 32, No. 1, March 1988, pp. 91-123. This study replicates one done in 1974 by Lloyd S. Etheredge and retests two hypotheses drawn from Interpersonal generalization theory to determine if the personality characteristics of dominance and extroversion-introversion crucially affect the policies advocated by American foreign policy elite.
9. Adopted from Robert J. Lieber, *No Common Power, Understanding IR* (Glenview: Scott, Foresman, 1988), p. 312.
10. Robert Gilpin, *War and Change in World Politics* (New York: Cambridge University Press, 1981).
11. See, for example, Kenneth A. Oye, "Constrained Confidence and the Evolution of Reagan Foreign Policy" in Lieber Oye, and Rothchild, eds., *Eagle Resurgent? The Reagan Era in American Foreign Policy* (Boston: Little, Brown, 1981).
12. Harold and Margaret Sprout, *Foundations of International Politics* (New York: Van Nostrand, 1963).
13. For use of the term "Hegemonic Stability," see Robert Keohane, "The Theory of Hegemonic Stability and Change in International Economic Regimes 1967-77" in Ole Hosti, R. Siverson, A. George, eds., *Change in the International System*, (Boulder: Westview, 1980).
14. See especially Charles P. Kindleberger, "Hierarchy versus Inertial Cooperation," *International Organization*, Autumn 1986, pp. 841-42.
15. Ezra Vogel, *Japan as Number One* (Cambridge, Mass: Harvard University Press, 1979).
16. Samuel P. Huntington, "The US Decline or Renewal?" *Foreign Affairs*, Winter 1988/89.
17. John P. Lovell, *Foreign Policy in Perspective: Strategy, Adoption, Decision Making* (New York: Holt, Rienhart and Winston, 1970), pp. 65-66.
18. Quoted in James Petras, "The World Market: Battleground for 1990s," *Economic and Political Weekly*, vol. XXV, no. 4, January 27, 1990.
19. Jean Jacques Rousseau, *The Social Contract* (London: J.M. Dent, 1947) Book III, Chap. XI, p. 73.

The Post-Cold War World Order: Some Emerging Trends

DILIP MOHITE

The end of cold war was received with a sign of relief by some, while others expressed apprehensions, especially the realist scholars who firmly believed in the merit of Hans Morgethau's classic balance of power theory. The collapse of Soviet Union left USA as the only superpower to monitor the fast moving complicated world events. Despite volatile situations in the third world countries, USA and the Soviet Union prevailed over their client states to refrain from conflict. Now, how far and how willing USA will be to exercise its muscle to maintain the world order? The emergence of regional powers with tremendous potential to manufacture nuclear bombs, missiles, chemical weapons, etc. are threatening to create fault lines almost all over the globe. Under the circumstances, this paper attempts to underline and analyze the factors which are likely to affect and influence the new world order.

End of the Bipolar World

The post-World War II scenario was marked by the emergence of two superpowers which maintained and played the classic balance of power game. Most realist writers on international politics subscribed to the view that such balance of power and bipolarity complimented each other and collectively secured the world from the outbreak of yet another large-scale war. The mutual deterrence theory also found sufficient scope in not only preventing confrontations between the two superpowers but also in exercising effective leverage on third world nations. The fear of possible involvement by either superpower prevented conflicts in the third world and also limited conflicts between the cold war protagonists to ideological differences only. As such, mutual deterrence saw the superpowers avoiding direct involvement in the third world states. In most cases, they resorted to proxy wars of which Vietnam and Afghanistan are classic examples.

1990 heralded the collapse of the Soviet Union and left USA as the only superpower with a unilateral control centre in the post-cold war era. The triumph of the US and her western capitalist allies left many experts interpreting this development as the emergence of a unipolar world. This was substantiated by the virtual hegemony of American interests in global affairs and also in international organizations such as the United Nations. American conduct in the recent Gulf War without resistance from any quarter is a pointer towards this trend.

Such behaviour also creates apprehensions regarding USA's motives to dictate or dominate the third world countries. A pertinent question therefore arises as to whether the third world has the capacity to shape its policies effectively in the face of the new danger or will it continue to remain fragmented and frustrated with its own internal conflicts? Internal cleavages in third world societies are the result of ethnic, religious, regional, linguistic and economic factors.[1]

Ethnic Conflicts

Most third world states are caught in the fray of ethnic conflicts and border disputes. There are several reasons for the prevalence of such domestic instability in third world societies. A key factor is the relative youth of the states. While it took Western Europe three to four centuries to develop a state and overcome the 'teething problems,' third world orders have had only three to four decades to inculcate a state identity among disparate groups and establish borders. Coupled with this is the legacy of colonialism as most third world states have been created by outside powers. Although the degree of correlation with existing ethnic outfits varies, almost all third world nations have had to deal with problems arising out of imposed borders, replacing flexible further divided ethnic groups by assigning them different tasks based on ethnicity, and by playing them off against each other. Due to the arbitrariness of their borders, most third world states remain artificial constructs rather than cohesive socio-political units. Moreover, there is no ethnic core in the third world to provide identity to the state. This is further complicated by the presence of several ethnic groups fighting for the control of the state or for the right to secede and establish their own state.[2] Building a cohesive state is also hampered by a lack of a common history and culture among different ethnic groups. Such ethnic fragmentation creates problems among states as well as within them.[3]

The inability to form strong states has led to internal warfare throughout the third world. Although obscured by the events of the Gulf War, most of the wars and threat to governments in the third world have domestic roots. Coup d'etat revolutions, insurgencies, and civil conflicts dominate the landscape of the third world. Recent or continuing internal conflicts have taken place in India, Afghanistan, Sri Lanka, Cambodia, Somalia, Ethiopia, Angola, Sudan, Chad, El Salvador, Guatemala, Peru, Nicaragua, Iraq, and several other third world states.[4] There is no indication that such third world conflicts will abate in the near future and hence, the regional threat to a new world order continues to persist.

To substantiate the above argument, it will be interesting to note that the most wars fought after II World War were fought in the third world. Out of 120 conflicts, 98 percent i.e. 118 were in the third world and 75 percent i.e. almost 90 out of 118 are between third world states and fourth world nations.[5]

The third world conflicts are over territory, not over politics or economics. Most of the states at war with nations are carrying out military invasions to annex territory and resources under the guise of national integration, nation building, border security, economic development, and eradication of "communist" or "terrorist." Most South Asian states are involved in this kind of conflict.

The goal of most nations is to regain or maintain local control over their territory, resources, peoples and communities. Military and political means are thereafter mobilized to achieve these goals. Sometimes, international political support and arms supply may be sought. For example, because Morocco is a staunch US ally in a strategic and otherwise anti-American region, King Massan II's twelve-year, million-dollar-per-day war against the Sahrawi Republic (Western Sahara) and its Polisario military is heavily supported by the US.

Environmental Degradation

It has also been suggested that environmental degradation in the third world countries accentuates the problem of ethnicity. Environmental degradation, particularly population pressure, whereby the land-man ratio as well as lack of economic opportunities leading to mass migration within or beyond the national boundaries, magnify ethnic conflicts and consequently, regional as well as global quest for order.[6] In many parts of the third world, agricultural land is being made barren due to droughts, silting of soil deforestation etc. This compels the starving masses to move towards tropical forests or hilly regions. Such migration to the "greener pastures" generates new hostilities of a domestic nature bordering on ethnic conflicts. The tension between India and Bangladesh on account of migration by Kurdish refugees etc. are examples of this trend.

The exploding population of the third world further complicates the attainment of political stability. In the third world of today, the population pressures forecast by Malthus are coming true, but the remedies that precluded disaster elsewhere are not available. Almost all projections predict much greater population growth in the third world societies and the population is doubling every twenty-five years.[7] In India, for example from 1968 to 1991, the population has grown from 530 million to 850 million. Growth rates, both globally, and in India, are still extraordinarily high: 2% per year and in the next thirty years, three billion people will be added to global population, including 435 million in India alone.[8] There are few signs that the third world will be able to cope with this explosive growth.

Environmental changes such as global warming, deforestation and topsoil erosion are adding to the dilemma. Such changes are likely to lead to reduced food production and economic decline. For example, the land hunger of an ever-increasing population has devastated the entire environment in Saurashtra (India) and brought about such disturbances of ecological system that land, man and beasts are equally at jeopardy.[9] Poor countries therefore, will experience low internal stability as governments lacking ability to deal with these multi-dimensional problems will resort to dictatorial control and increased repression. Externally, increased warfare among third world states can be expected due to conflicts over natural resources such as clean water and fertile land. Conflicts may also increase between third world and non-third world nations as the third world attempts to redress the growing gap in living standards exacerbated by the impact of the environment.[10]

Economic Policies

The only hope for stability in the third world lies in greater economic development of the region. Putting aside for the moment the uncertain future of at least some of the newly industrialized countries (NICs) such as Hong Kong and South Korea, the prospect that many third world countries will emulate industrial development of the NICs is low. Generating wealth by exporting to the developed states is extremely difficult due to a slackening of global demand for goods produced in the third world and increased protectionism in economic sectors where the third world does well (e.g. textiles). Developing high technology industries is also difficult due to the lack of an educational base in most third world nations. The declining costs of raw materials, especially when compared with manufactured goods, and the diminishing role played by labour in the cost of goods further impedes third world economic development. Moreover, it is now argued that the success of Asian NICs has much to do with the fact that they are all "strong states" – a missing ingredient throughout much of the third world.[11]

Diffusion of Military Capability from North to South

As military competition between the two superpowers gradually slowed down, "low-intensity conflict" has become a dominant military motif of the 1990s. Internal wars, border struggles, police actions and other types of "bushfire" combat represents the principal form of conflict in the post-cold war world and is likely to remain so in the foreseeable future. But while low-intensity warfare may predominate, there is a growing risk of what might be called "mid-intensity conflict" – warfare involving the large and medium powers of the third world. These regional hegemonies possess most of the modern weapons supplied to the third world and boast a virtual monopoly over the third world's nuclear and chemical weapon arsenal, over the past twenty years. An all-out military encounter between such countries is bound to have far-reaching global repercussions. The likely violence of such encounters is partly a result of the international arms flow. While many third world nations participated in an orgy of arms buying beginning in the mid-seventies, a dozen or so countries wound up with the lion's share of these weapons. This fearsome trend was amply demonstrated during the prolonged Iran-Iraq conflict, which produced an estimated 1,250,000 casualities and escalated to widespread use of chemical weapons and ballistic missiles against civilian populations.[12]

It is estimated that during the eighties, the third world countries produced arms, ammunition and combat-related items worth 350 billion from the industrial powers of the North. These included 11,000 tanks and self-propelled howitzers, 20,000 artillery pieces, 3,100 supersonic jet flighters, 37,000 surface-to-air missiles, and 540 warships and submarines. The Stockholm International Peace Research Institute (SIPRI) yearbook for 1989 reports that three-quarters of the major weapons transferred to the third world between 1984 and 1988 ended up in only fourteen nations: Angola, Egypt, India, Iran, Iraq, Israel, Libya, North Korea, Pakistan, Saudi Arabia, South Korea, Syria, Taiwan, and Turkey.[13] A more recent trend among third world countries is not only the procurement of finished products but also of technology to produce arms in their own countries. While forty or so nations now produce some sort of light weaponry and ammunition, about ten third world countries possess a significant military-industrial infrastructure. These include Egypt, India, Israel, North Korea, South Korea, and Taiwan as major arms exporters plus Argentina, Brazil, China and South Africa as heavy investors in domestic military production.

Apart from importing and exporting sophisticated weaponry, the third world states have recently started developing military technical skill with a view to integrate these weapons into a professional military set-up and to use them effectively in regional conflicts. As the importance of such skills is being realized, greater emphasis is laid on rapid communication, sophisticated surveillance systems and computer-based technology. Furthermore, a large number of military personnel from the third world have been trained in the sophisticated environs of the USA, Great Britain, France, (former) Soviet Union and Israel. America alone has trained nearly one and a half million soldiers from the third world and has often undertaken extensive bilateral military exercises in several third world countries. (For example, the joint Indo-US naval exercise conducted in 1992). All such developments augment the likelihood (as also frequency and intensity) of regional conflicts in the third world, most noticeably by way of ushering in a 'regional arms race.' The Iran-Iraq, India and Pakistan have also entered into a localized arms race which threatens to erupt into a nuclear conflict. There are certain calculable as well as incalculable effects of a nuclear war between India and Pakistan. According to S. Rashid Naim, any use of nuclear weapons in the region, even on a small and limited scale, would cause very high civilian casualities and collateral damage. It would be likely to cause escalation from a limited nuclear exchange into a major counter-strike on cities. Among the expected effects of the nuclear war that cannot be calculated would be irreversible changes in the weather pattern and environment, mutations in plant and animal life, and unpredictable changes in the social and political order.[14] In fact, there are certain political and social factors peculiar to the South Asian region which are likely to affect casualities and destruction after the nuclear war. These include the "soft" nature of both India and Pakistan as states, and in the case of India, communal violence. Both states have within their borders linguistic and ethnic minorities which may not share war objectives and may see in the destruction caused by the war a chance to break away from the state. Regional and ethnic tensions are also likely to be exacerbated by disagreement over the regional priority in allocation of scarce resources for recovery. Although in more economically developed countries post-attack casualties could be limited by relying on medical shelter and economic resources of smaller allies, this would not be possible in the case of India and Pakistan. It is also impossible for either country to undertake an effective post-attack recovery without massive external assistance. And finally, it is conceivable that political crisis following a nuclear exchange may lead to the break-up and disintegration of both India and

Pakistan. Keeping these points in mind, it must be remembered that the acquisition of nuclear weapons by India and Pakistan will eventually lead to instability in South Asia. Thus, if nuclear weapons are ever to be introduced into the region, it is imperative that this introduction be gradual and symmetrical and that the conditions necessary for a credible and robust deterrence be established.

Implications of These Trends

The emergence of the new elite power structure comprising certain nations of the third world has great significance for the future evolution of a global system. These new regional powers are:

Africa:	Algeria, Angola, Egypt, Libya and South Africa.
Middle East:	Iran, Iraq, Israel, Saudi Arabia, Syria and Turkey.
South Asia:	India and Pakistan.
East Asia:	China, North Korea, South Korea and Taiwan.

In addition to this, Chile, Thailand and Indonesia are likely to join the group by the mid-nineties. This entire configuration will affect North-South relations as well as inter-state relations within the region. Interactions between these nations are likely to lead to serious military and political implications for the rest of the world as well.

The most significant consideration to be kept in mind is that within this group of twenty nations, most are engaged in mutually antagonistic relationships with each other. These rivalries develop into arms race and create war-like situation of a highly volatile nature. Pairings of this type include India-Pakistan, India-China, Egypt-Israel, Egypt-Libya, Syria-Iraq, Israel-Syria, Iran-Iraq, China-Taiwan and North Korea-South Korea. It may be noted that these pairings have been responsible for a majority of inter-state conflicts, not only in the third world but also in the entire world of the post-World War II era.

The immediate offshoot of such a conflictual scenario is the drain of limited economic resources of the already underdeveloped third world countries, resulting in rising debt burdens and greater economic instability. From a related viewpoint, while it is known that an increasing number of third world countries are attempting to substitute domestically manufactured arms for imported ones, the extent of their success in actually reducing dependence on the great powers of the world is negligible. Hence, a regional arms race also entails greater economic as well as military dependence on the developed countries. The fragility of a domestic economy tends to encourage social and political disorder in almost every third world country. Ethnicity and separatist tendencies in several underdeveloped nations have been directly attributed to a negligence of government which is so engrossed in international power struggles that it fails to solve national problems effectively. This is the typical "weak state" characteristic which has been explained by Barry Buzan as a nation which has 'failed to create a domestic political and social consensus of sufficient strength to eliminate the largescale use of force as a major and continuing element in the domestic political life of that nation.'[15] This is indeed, a central feature of most third world countries and contributes substantially towards creating an "insecurity dilemma" in the region. So, they have to face the realities of a more or less anarchic international system (especially in the post-cold war era) and yet, strive to survive within it while simultaneously accommodating their internal conflicts. This dilemma worsens neighbouring antagonistic states begin to interfere with each other's domestic polity with a view to destabilize it. The Pakistan-sponsored state terrorism and insurgency movements in India are a well-known example of a regional "cold war" which has been rendered highly volatile due to indirect means of confrontation adopted by one of the warring states. Examples of India-China, India-Sri Lanka and Iran-Iraq can also be quoted in this context. Emerging nuclear capabilities of some of these nations only make the situation more dangerous.

Yet, the military implications of these emerging regional patterns are debatable. On the one hand, the supporters of the mutual deterrence theory argue that the possibility of war will decrease in the future, basically due to greater and more sophisticated arming of the third world states. As the theory worked with relative success between the United States and the Soviet Union during the cold war era, similar logic may apply to newer powers in the post-cold war era. For instance, eminent Indian scholar K. Subrahmanyam has argued time and again that a regional mutual deterrence and fear of deadly after-effects of a nuclear fall-out alone prevent India and Pakistan from resorting to a direct confrontation now. On the other hand, there are those who highlight the limitations of the mutual deterrence theory and quoting the example of the 1967 Cuban Missile Crisis when the world was on the brink of a nuclear disaster, explain how this theory is not fool proof. These adherents argue that the end of the cold war has not reduced the threat of regional conflict, especially when considered in the light of emerging challenges from nuclear proliferation. As more and more third world nations acquire nuclear capability and delivery systems such as ballistic missiles, the mutual deterrence theory weakens considerably. Hence, factors like increased intensity of mutual regional conflicts, greater accidents and immaturity of the underdeveloped third world nations tend to complicate the scenario. It can also be argued that while the third world might still hesitate to use nuclear weapons, it is certainly not inhibited in the use of chemical weapons. Iran and Iraq abundantly used chemical weapons during the long-drawn war between them which resulted in unprecedented loss of lives and property. Saddam Hussain of Iraq has time and again threatened to use chemical weapons against his opponents. The Pakistan President in recent times has reserved the right of first strike nuclear attack on India. Therefore, one cannot rule out the use of these weapons, and perhaps, of more lethal ones, in the near future. This again brings in the inter-relatedness between internal and external conflicts of the third world. The Kurdish movement in Iraq, the Intifada in Israel, the fundamentalist movements in India etc. increase the chances of both internal as well as external conflicts in these multi-ethnic societies and very often, augur the use of highly destructive weapons therein. All these issues must come in for serious consideration in the evolution of a new world order. Instability in the third world can also be attributed to legacies of colonialism (which nurture ethnicity and strong nationalist tendencies), religious fervour (due to widespread illiteracy) and massive public support (in the form of militarism and hypernationalism). Thus, security becomes a major issue not only for a particular region but for the world at large.

End of Superpower Intervention in the Third World?

Originally, the US-Soviet rivalry for domination and control over various parts of the world was limited to Europe and the Far East. Gradually however, this competition led to a heavy concentration of conventional forces in these regions, with a high risk of nuclear fallout. Therefore, the third world came into the picture as a hitherto unexploited "power vacuum." It was seen as a blank gameboard on which both the superpowers moved their pieces in the competition for strategic advantage. Each tried to assess its opponent's strength on the gameboard by accounting for each other's capabilities, priorities, moves and countermoves. In 1990 however, the Soviet Union withdrew most of its pieces off the gameboard in order to conserve resources for the rejuvenation of its domestic economy. But despite the end of the cold war, its after-effects continue to remain major irritants in the quest for a new global order. It has often been felt that the world will continue to witness occasional forays by the most powerful nations of the world against allies and proxies of their respective opponents. In fact, most of the developed nations continue covert aggressions against their adversaries by retaining allies in the underdeveloped third world, especially by way of supplying arms and military technology. USA for example, continuously supplied weapons to Israel, Saudi Arabia and Pakistan, while Russia promoted similar trends in India, Algeria, Iraq and Syria. Since both Moscow and Washington have attempted to establish long-term alliances with the emerging regional powers, they have repeatedly acceded to demands of their clients for access to increasingly sophisticated arms. Mutually reinforcing power struggles have also contributed to the proliferation of nuclear and chemical weapons in the third world. To quote an instance, in order to insure Pakistan's cooperation in the secret US effort to arm the Afghan Mujaheddin, the Reagan administration had repeatedly overlooked Pakistan's nuclear weapons programme, and the present administration failed to declare Pakistan as a state sponsoring terrorism despite incriminating evidence provided by India. The US also responded timidly to the Israeli and Chinese nuclear programmes while the Soviets looked the other way as Iraq and Libya acquired chemical weapons.[16] Furthermore, the US behaviour in this respect has been rationalized on the grounds that losing third world allies will adversely affect its economic interests (such as the growth of multinationals and the supply of oil). Richard L. Armitage warned those critics who predicted America's decline that the Gulf war has amply demonstrated how "the United States alone possesses sufficient moral, economic, political and military horse-power to jump start and drive international efforts to curb international lawlessness."[17]

Also Charles William Maynes explains that in the nineties, "the United States will have a strong interest in trying to build firebreaks between the local conflicts in the third world and the great powers, to promote conventional arms control among third world countries, and to strengthen prohibitions on the future proliferation of chemical and nuclear weapons."[18]

It is thus, being increasingly realized that despite the apparent unipolarity of the existing international system, regional issues continue to dominate the global agenda. For example, the US can no longer remain unconcerned about the third world's military advances considering recent acquisition of long-range (inter-continental) ballistic missiles and lethal arsenal with tremendous strike capability. Moreover, American interests are spread over almost all the regions of the world. From another perspective, the invincibility of USA has also been challenged; it has been argued that success in the Gulf War was a concerted effort of several western powers (under the American/United Nations' aegis) against just one regional power. A concert of more than two regional powers or simultaneous resistance to USA and its allies can indeed, have serious repercussions on global order.

At the same time however, it is heartening to realize that such dangerous situations are not likely to arise in the near future. The effect of the collapse of the Soviet Union, ethnic conflicts all across the world, and the triumph of "good over evil" in the Gulf War will linger on for quite sometime. This should stonewall any attempts at adventurism on the parts of rising regional powers of the post-cold war world.

Therefore, it can be concluded that the post-cold war world order is truly a classic case of uncertainty. The certainty is that the world will be free from most of the complications of the cold war while the uncertainty is that the world will continue to become increasingly anarchic and disorderly.

NOTES

1. Mohammed Ayoob, "Regional Security and the Third World," *Regional Conflict and Global Security in the 1990s*, Centre for International Cooperation and Security Studies (Madison: University of Wisconsin, 1990), p. 39.
2. Urmila Phadnis, *Ethnicity and Nation Building in South Asia* (New Delhi: Sage, 1989), p. 28.
3. Stephen Cohen, "The State is Dead: Long Live the Armed Ethnic Group."
4. Steven R. David, "Why the Third World still Matters," *International Security*, vol. 17, no. 3, Winter 1992/93, pp. 131-34.
5. *Ibid.*
6. Nahid Islam, "Ethnicity and Environment in South Asia," *Bangladesh and SAARC: Issues, Perspectives and Outlook*, ed. Iftekharuzzaman and Imtiaz Ahmed (Dhaka: Academic Publishers, 1992), p. 41.
7. Nicholas Eberstadt, "Population Change and National Security," *Foreign Affairs*, vol. 70, no. 3, Summer 1919, pp. 117-18.
8. Robert McNamara, "A Global Population to Advance Human Development in the 21st Century, with Particular Reference to India," The Rajiv Gandhi Memorial Lecture, New Delhi, May 23, 1992.
9. M.N. Buch, "Population and Environment in Science," *Population and Development*, ed. Vasant Gowarikar (Pune: Umesh Communications, 1992), p. 95.

10. Steven R. David, pp. 141-52.
11. *Ibid*,. pp. 140-41.
12. Michael T. Klare, "Wars in the 1990s: Growing Fire Powers in the Third World" (Chicago: Educational Foundation for Nuclear Science, 1990), p. 2.
13. SIPRI Year Book, Stockholm, 1989.
14. S. Rashid Naim, "After Midnight," *Nuclear Proliferation in South Asia*, ed. Stephen P. Cohen (USA: Westview Press, 1991), pp. 29-60.
15. From Brian L. Job, "The Insecurity Dilemma: National, Regime and State Securities in the Third World."
16. Michael T. Klare, p. 291.
17. *Ibid*.
18. C.W. Maynes, "America's Third World Hang-ups," *Foreign Policy*, no. 71, Summer 1988, p. 133.

The End of the Cold War and New Challenges to USA

B. K. GUPTA

Former USSR President Mikhail Gorbachev's programmes of perestroika and glasnost had started putting nails in the coffin of the cold war and the disintegration of the erstwhile USSR brought the end of the burial rites of the cold war. As a result of this the former USSR lost its status of being a super power and USA has remained a lone super power in the world. With this situation the old blocs and the blocism is almost nonexistent now. The ideological differences, too, have declined as with the fall of communist governments in eastern Europe and with failure of communism in the former USSR, people are disillusioned with communism and its myth of greenery. With this background scenario a new world order is in the offing.

Whatever be the world opinion about communism, Marxism has created awareness about the exploitation. All over the world people have opoosed colonialism, hegemony and exploitation of all sorts. Also, Marxism has created a sense of internationalism by giving a call to the workers all over the world to unite.

In the light of these facts, as a lone super power in the world, USA is to confront new challenges in the new world order—economic and political—that is emerging quite fast and with its thrust. With the end of cold war the world heaved a sigh of relief hoping for enduring peace in the days to come. But the peace appears to be only a mirage.

The following are the new challenges which USA has to confront with.

Trust-building

What the new trends in the world suggest is that it is going to become only one world. This nonscientific division of the globe into three worlds is about to disappear. The only need is its careful handling and being a super power and resourceful country, USA may take lead in this stride.

For this, USA will have to endeavour to create an atmosphere of trust-building in order to remove all sorts of apprehensions among the different countries of the world. North Korea's withdrawal from NPT recently may be seen in this light. The news items like "US plan to neutralise India" (*The Hindustan Times*, 17 March 1991, p. 15) are deterimental to the process of trust-building as the international relations depend and base on mutual trust and faith and mutual interest. No amount of good diplomacy can help it if such apprehensions are once allowed to develop.

International Terrorism

Recent bomb explosions both in India and USA are indications that both the countries are in the grip of international terrorism. Some Islamic countries are known to be hostile and inimical to USA, e.g., Iran, Iraq, and Libya. Some more states are suspected to have joined their ranks. So is the case with India. Hence India will have to be strong militarily in the presence of such threats. The USA should not only perceive it but help India. Both the countries can cooperate and help each other. Of late, there was a call given to the Muslims all over the world as the caption to the news item reads "Muslims urged to unite against west." (*The Hindustan Times*, 14 March 1993) Not only this, Arab countries appealed to the member countries of NAM to consider immediately the likely danger of Unipolar world as it may endanger the sovereignty of the developing countries. It may be seen as a direct challenge to USA since it is the only super power in the world now.

International Trade

The economy which the present US administration has got in sucession is not in a very good state. So, the international trade is another new challenge before USA. Super 301 and Dunkel proposals have come in for severe criticism especially in the underdeveloped countries. Protectionism will not help USA. More trade is the only solution. Mutual interests, not the self interest will have to be kept in mind as a core of foreign policy otherwise what will happen all over the world is that different trade zones will come into existence. Say, for example, European community. Japan is trying to develop a trade zone with Asian countries. Iran is trying to woo India with an intention "to prevent domination of the central Asian republics by big powers." (*The Hindustan Times*, 12 March 1993) An appeal for the new global trade deserves attention. "A group of 37 nations has appealed to the United States, Japan and Europe to agree on a new global trade accord to help reverse Global Economic decline." (*The Hindustan Times*, 14 March 1993) Argentine President Carlos Saul Menem, spokesman for the group said "the accord will also help countries like Argentina that have been liberalising their trade laws and should take into account the needs of the world's poorest countries." (*Ibid.*) Actually "What the Third World needs more than anything else is trade and not so-called aid which is often tied with political and other strings. What the Third World needs is fair terms for trade without tariff and quota barriers."[1]

If USA has some trade problems with Japan and China as these countries have trade surplus, it can be sorted out by having bilateral talks with them. Protectionism or Dunkel proposals or/to impose tough terms on developing and under-developed countries will not help in solving the problem. Exploitation-tactics or measures will not be tolerated. They are now anachronistic and also they would not be commensurating with the American philosophy of liberty, freedom and free institutions.

Though communism has failed yet Marxism has created awareness about the exploitation. Exploitation in any form will invite opposition and resentment. Capitalism has to improve its face. There is no question of hegemony. Hegemony, too, will not be tolerated. Only the equality in exercise and practice will help the situation.

N.P.T.

N.P.T. has been another issue between USA and the developing countries. As it has been discussed earlier the success of NPT will depend on mutual trust. Intimidation or brow-beating or strong arm tactics will not be able to achieve the desired results. It should be fresh in memory that during the gulf war USA has threatened to use a nuclear weapon against Iraq and it was widely condemned. The latest case of North Korea's withdrawal from NPT should be again an eye-opener. It was reported in the print media that "Pyongyang said it would remain outside the treaty until United States stops its nuclear threats against North Korea." (*The Hindustan Times*, 13 March 1993, p.14) If it is the fact, then North Korea's stand is not objectionable. Another news item is equally important and deserves attention to it. It reads "NPT major irritant in Indo-US ties." (*The Hindustan Times*, 10 March 1993) Two well known American professors and foreign policy experts, who visited Calcutta earlier this month (i.e. March) "identified the two major irritants in US-India relations at present, namely, the nuclear non-proliferation treaty and the missile technology." (*Ibid.*) It means, according to them, the issues of Super 301 and the Dunkel proposals are not that much . .

. serious issues between the two countries if India signs NPT. "Both, however, agreed that the geopolitical realities involving India and Pakistan would continue to influence the US options, with distinct possibilities of India making for further gains in the US perception." (*Ibid.*)

Another point also deserves a mention here. A report submitted recently to the US-Congress on "South Asia: US Interests and Policy Issues" prepared by specialists in foreign and Asian Affairs, Mr. Richard P. Cronin and Ms. Barbara Leitch Lepoer, and made available in New Delhi points out, inter alia, that "China is not a promising candidate for any accord that would contain its own nuclear arsenal or even, it would seem, its restraint in regard to missile and nuclear technology exports. A Chinese guarantee not to use nuclear weapons against India would have a tough time achieving credibility in New Delhi, the specialists note." (*The Hindustan Times*, 24 March 1993, p. 17) Even then, not only Bush Administration but also President Clinton is of the opinion to continue 'Most Favoured Nation' status of China. Now, these facts are self-speaking. The idea is that India's not signing NPT should not be an irritant in the ties between the two countries, particularly, in the light of other pressing problems such as those of economy and international trade and international terrorism.

Liberalisation

Most of the countries in the world have only one type of economic model i.e. open market competitive economic model, switching on to liberalization of their economy. Communist or socialist model of economy has totally failed. Not only this, people all over the world now hate it. The latest French elections stand witness. USA should not do anything so the sense of exploitation should get strengthened and communism may get a chance to revive. Some theoreticians believe that Karl Marx proved to be true as he had predicted that counter-revolution might take place. So there is a possibility of counter-revolution to this. Thus, there is a danger of revival of communism. The problems before the Russian President Boris Yeltsin, posed by the hard-liners in his country may be seen in this light.

Human Rights

The question of human rights is also another challenging issue. The issue of human rights too should not be raked in such a way as it might be taken as political interference in that country's internal affairs. The question of human rights is very ticklish and sensitive. It would not be liked by a self-respecting nation. Tackling of terrorism and secessionism with firmness and iron-hand should not be taken to be a violation of human rights. A genuine difference in the light of ground realities is to be made. Particulalry in case of a country like India whose unfriendly neighbors are creating problems for it by helping terrorism and secession in India in many a way. The US administration is itself getting more and more convinced about it.

The recent visit of Mr. John Malott to India in May 93 has left behind a bad taste in mouth and a sense of bitterness in the official as well as private circles. The press reports in print media in India show that the BJP and leftist parties took serious exception to the statements made by Mr. John Malott, among other things, regarding human rights violation in Kashmir.

One fails to understand why the US administration is so concerned and vociferous in raking up the issue of human rights violation only in Indian part of Kashmir. They never talk about situation of human rights in Pak occupied Kashmir (POK). Is the condition of human rights in POK ideal or any better than that in the Indian part of Kashmir?

In respect of human rights, terrorists, militants and insurgents and their accomplices cannot be put or treated on par with civilians or common citizens since the former are the groups of law-breakers and secessionists while the latter are a law-abiding and peace-loving lot. A genuine distinction between the two will have to be made.

Mr. John Malott has been reported to have admitted: "The US is well aware that Indian security forces in Kashmir are operating under very difficult circumstances. It also knew that some of the statistics of abuses were wildly exaggerated. What we do not know is the truth about how much, how many, how often, or who and that is not only in Kashmir, but also in other situations around the world." (*The Hindustan Times*, 14 June 1993, p. 1) It has also been reported that "The US is aware and has publicly stated that the militants are also committing human rights violations." (*Ibid.*)

What is, then, the source of Mr. Malott's information when he himself admits that they do not know the truth? Their source of information appears to be only the malicious and vilifying propaganda against India by the parties that are hostile to her and have their vested interest in such a propaganda. Then, how far is it justified to ignore India's official view and version and to give credibility to the version of known India-baiters, pro-Khalistanis, pro-JKLF and others of their ilk?

The recently concluded UN world conference on human rights, held in Vienna (Austria) should be able to provide an opportunity to the US administration to give a second thought to the plank of human right of its foreign policy. The present US administration should think as to how the third world countries look at its human rights policy. In this conference, as per the reports received from Vienna, the West's stand on human was termed and criticised by the developing nations as interference smacking of imperialism." (*The Hindustan Times*, 16 June 1993, p. 22) Also, according to Mr. Samuel Huntington, head of the Olin Institute for Strategic Studies at Harvard University, "The more militant Asians, of course, attack America for "human rights imperialism." (*The Hindustan Times*, 18 June 1993, p. 14)

Another report from Vienna conference itself equally deserves attention. "Several Asian countries, including Malaysia and Indonesia, argued that as long as Western nations continued to preach morality while practising hypocrisy, human rights will be used as a stick to beat up developing nations." (*The Hindustan Times*, 20 June 1993, p. 24)

In this context a political analyst's view on Mr. John Malott's comments on India/human rights is quite important to be taken note of. "Those who have listened to Mr. John Malott's admonition about human rights with due difference know very well that the bite in his words comes not from the moral authority of the nation on whose behalf he speaks but from its military and economic power."[2]

In the Vienna world conference on Human Rights Dalai Lama, a Nobel Peace Prize Winner, was not given entry to it. Tibetans' human rights case could not be discussed in the conference simply because China did not want it. Then, why should India allow any country to raise the issue of human rights in Indian part of Kashmir?

By citing all these reports and views the sole idea is that the US administration will have to set in order its own records on international morality and will have to prove its genuine concern for human rights all over the world instead of using them as a ploy to interfere in the internal affairs of others. America's raising human rights issue in other countries should not look like an interventionist tactics. Then only USA can become a real champion of human rights in the world.

Use of Force

The past experience stands witness that the measure of use of force to solve a problem has failed. Rather it has created a lot of problems to be tackled and solved later. Recent case of Gulf war should be an eye-opener. Iraq and Libya could not be subdued by the use of force. Not only this, there was a news item that appeared in print media in India that "Iraq 'funded' World Trade Centre blast" (*The Hindustan Times*, 26 March 1993, p. 14) in New York in the month of February.

Strengthening of Democracy in the World

Strengthening of democraccy in the world is another challenging issue but the democracy should be strengthened through the UNO. Local or regional conflicts should be solved by using the platform of the UNO by democratic means. The USA should not involve itself directly as it may be taken to be American imperialist or hegemonistic tactics.

Question of Universalism

A sense of universalism that is universal belongingness, or a sense of mutual interdependence should be created and strengthened. A sense of universalism, not the sense of regionalism or sectarianism, seems to be the only solution to make the world conflict-free.

NOTES

1. T.N. Kaul, "Perestroika and the Third World," *The Hindustan Times*, 2 Feb. 1990, p. 11.
2. Sham Lal, "The International Scene—How the Past Lingers on," *The Times of India*, 22 May 1993, p. 8.

Index